We Are a People in This World

We Are a People in This World

THE LAKOTA SIOUX AND THE MASSACRE AT WOUNDED KNEE

Conger Beasley Jr.

THE UNIVERSITY OF ARKANSAS PRESS
FAYETTEVILLE 1995

02 01 00 99 98   5 4 3 2

Designed by John Coghlan

⊛ The paper used in this publication meets the minimum requirements of the
American National Standard for Permanence of Paper for Printed Library
Materials Z39.48-1984.

Library of Congress Cataloging-in-Publication Data

Beasley, Conger.
    We are a people in this world : the Lakota Sioux and the massacre at
Wounded Knee / Conger Beasley, Jr.
    p.   cm.
    Includes bibliographical references.
    ISBN 1-55728-387-7 (alk. paper). — ISBN 1-55728-386-9 (pbk. : alk.
paper)
    1. Wounded Knee Massacre, S.D., 1890—Personal narratives. 2. Dakota
Indians—History—19th century. 3. Dakota Indians—Social life and
customs. I. Title.
E83.89.B43   1995
973.8'6–dc20
                                                                94-48101
                                                                CIP

For the people of the Lakota Nation

Mitakuye oyasin

Acknowledgments

The author would like to thank the following people for their assistance in the research and writing of this book: Pinky Plume, Dooch Clifford, Dana Garber, Ted Hamilton, Doris Giago, Eileen Fallon, Guy Mount, Sandra Hoffman, and Glenda McCrary.

The author would also like to thank Alex White Plume, one of the original Big Foot Memorial riders, for his invaluable help in identifying and correcting errors of fact and interpretation. Any faults the book may have, either as historical record or contemporary narrative, are solely the responsibility of the author.

1

The country rivaled Siberia in the severity of its winters.

—*Julia B. McGillycuddy,* Blood on the Moon: Valentine McGillycuddy and the Sioux *(1941)*

West of Valentine, on a lonely winter road, I saw my first sundog. It was the afternoon of the December solstice. The sun hanging in the western sky had fractured into a trio of lemony orbs that hovered just above the horizon. I took my foot off the accelerator and let the car glide down toward a bridge where a half-dozen cattle huddled next to the icy surface of a stock pond. A mass of dark air draped the sky like a shroud; the effect on the sun's rays was prismatic, refracting the rays into identical suns that glimmered at the edges of the shroud. Inside the car, with the tape deck churning out the calypso rhythms of the Neville Brothers, the atmosphere was cozy and warm. Outside, tufted with clumps of brittle grass, the snowy humps of the Sand Hills undulated toward a distant horizon. The grass poking through the snow was delicately touched with a pastel light. The shadows between the hills were tinged with a violet depth. Despite the severity of the temperature, the bleakness of the hills, the landscape looked as lovely as a Renoir canvas.

In Gordon, Nebraska, an hour later, the digital clock over the front door of the Great Plains National Bank indicated the temperature was seventeen degrees below zero. The streets were packed with snow, the air dry and still. I got out of the car to pump some gas and felt my fingers stick to the metal nozzle of the hose. A burning sensation gripped my hands. When I tried to pocket the change from the cashier, the bills slipped to the floor. Cars passed along the streets with a muffled crunch. The pressure of the cold was like an invisible screw that tightened against the town, pinching everything into a cramped and tiny space.

It was another hour before the car glided down a hill into the hamlet of Wounded Knee, on the Pine Ridge Indian Reservation, across the border in South Dakota. Lights winked from a scattering of lonely houses. I missed the Manderson turnoff and had to wheel the car around the battered historical marker located at the foot of a prominent hill on top of which, a hundred years ago, scores of Lakota men, women, and children had been unceremoniously dumped after dying in a hail of fire from Seventh Cavalry troops. In the headlights' glare I noticed that the word "Battle" in the title had been hammered over with a board marked "Massacre." I braked the car to a halt and shut off the lights. The dark at the foot of the hill was as impenetrable as engine oil. It seemed to lap over the car like a wave, engulfing the doors, sealing the windows. I tapped two fingers against the steering wheel. In the summer of 1983 I picked up a hitchhiker near this spot. His name was Rudy Pretty Hip. Rudy was forty years old, and he had only one leg. With difficulty he poked his crutch into the back seat; ducking to wedge himself inside, he knocked off his hat and hit his head. The smell of cheap wine filled the car like a rank perfume. A few minutes later, passing on the road below the hill and the grave site, Rudy broke into a fit of sobbing and buried his puffy face in his hands. From the front seat my wife reached back and tried to comfort him. I slowed the car and looked around helplessly. Rudy claimed he had lost the leg in Vietnam. "I saw my buddies get shot down like dogs," he choked through a flood of tears. "Like those people buried up there."

His grief was inconsolable. Reaching behind the front seat at an awkward angle, I tried to touch him and ended up running my fingers along the shaft of his crutch. It was as if someone had turned a spigot, triggering a gusher, tapping a deep fount of sorrow. A shudder racked his body; with an effort he finally composed himself. He sat straight up in the back seat, staring out through the front windshield, his face set in an impassive mask. A few minutes later, at the turnoff to Pine Ridge, he clambered wordlessly out of the car. A stiff wind rippled the tips of the lush grass bordering the road. Rudy clamped the hat down on his head and swung on his crutch to the other side of the road and planted himself on the gravel shoulder, ready to thumb a ride to Gordon, Nebraska. He didn't say goodbye. He didn't look over as I steered the car down the road toward Pine Ridge.

I continued to tap my fingers against the steering wheel as the car idled alongside the battered historical marker in the profound gloom of the darkest and coldest winter night I could remember. What had happened to Rudy? I wondered. Was he still alive? After the incident, an Oglala friend told me that Rudy hadn't lost a leg in Vietnam; he passed out on a railroad track outside Gordon and a locomotive ran over his leg. An icy wind rattled the car on the rubbery mounts of its wheels. I sat in the dark a few moments, then turned on the lights, shifted into gear, and went looking for Manderson Road.

On a yellow school bus the following afternoon, packed with Oglala children and teenagers, we bumped north through the Badlands toward Bridger, South Dakota. From Bridger the next morning, the second week of *Sitanka Wokiksuye*, the Big Foot Memorial Ride would begin. Three hundred riders, walkers, and support people were expected to join in. (I had made an arrangement with a man by telephone to rent a horse, but looking out at the bleak Badlands terrain through the bus window I began to question the sanity of that notion.) The object of the ceremony was to retrace the original path that Big Foot's band of Miniconjous had taken a hundred years earlier as they fled the Cheyenne River Reservation after Sitting Bull's death. The journey would begin on the morning of December 23 and end on the afternoon of the twenty-eighth, when the participants converged on Wounded Knee. Each December for the past four years a group of riders and walkers had retraced the journey. The first year, 1986, nineteen riders and one support vehicle had made the trip.

Constructed of drab concrete, looking more like a fortification than an education center, the Takini School of the Cheyenne River Reservation a few miles north of Bridger was jammed that night with crowds of Indians and *wasicu*. Media from both the United States and Europe were present: men with beards, women with long hair, both snugly dressed in bulky winter clothes, cameras looped around shoulders, notebooks prominently in hand.

A press information officer briefed us as to what we could and could not record. All religious ceremonies were off limits; we could not photograph the riders whenever they circled around the drummers and medicine men, whether in the morning before departing or in the evening before dismounting. The circle was *wakan*, or holy. We nodded solemnly and signed the releases. Members of the European media far outnumbered their North American counterparts. They were also more splendidly garbed in leather pants, buckskin shirts, buffalo-hide coats, and wide-brimmed hats banded with turquoise medallions.

By seven o'clock people thronged the floor of the Takini gym. Two maintenance men rolled the portable bleachers folded against the wall like an accordion out to the edge of the basketball court; the tiers were quickly occupied with men, women, and children spread out on blankets and bedrolls, nestled in the troughs between the wooden benches. A Shaking of the Hands Ceremony brought scores of people to the floor where they formed a double circle with the head of the outside line attaching itself to the tail of the inside, the two lines forming a kind of interlocking helix that went on and on in a procession of cordial greetings. The event was meticulously recorded by the media. Flashbulbs popped; cameramen moved in at oblique angles to capture the expressions of people greeting one another with handshakes; technicians with headsets and recorders pushed microphones into the faces of anyone willing to talk.

The *Ichecunza*, or Making of the Vows Ceremony, followed. Those riders and walkers, Indian and *wasicu*, intending to trace Big Foot's path from Bridger to Wounded Knee stepped forward and removed an eagle feather from the sacred hoop. By taking the feather they committed themselves to the journey. No matter the weather, no matter the hardship, once the feather was taken the walker or rider was honor bound to follow the trip to the end. It was a solemn moment, sanctified by prayers, accompanied by a media blackout. Proctors moved through the crowd making sure all cameras were properly capped or turned away. The dozen Indians standing in the center of the gymnasium floor included several of the original riders who had participated in the first *Sitanka Wokiksuye* in 1986. A tall, distinguished man in his late thirties named Arvol Looking Horse held the hoop to which the eagle feathers were attached. Arvol, a Miniconjou from the Cheyenne River Reservation, would figure prominently in the events of the next few days. His family for many generations had been the keepers of the sacred pipe, holiest of Lakota artifacts. Arvol had a dangling queue of glossy hair, the swarthy oval face of a full blood. For the entire hour it took to complete the ceremony, he stood rock-still, staring straight ahead, barely acknowledging the people who stepped forward to untie their feathers.

An honoring song in memory of Sitting Bull followed the taking of the vows. Eight men squeezed knee to knee around a drum flailed away at the taut skin with leather-tipped sticks; their voices in quavery unison rose to the raftered ceiling in a high-pitched lament. A pained expression crimped the drummers' faces. A sharp, accented wail issued from high up in their throats; people standing behind them closed their eyes and mouthed the words and rocked back and forth on their heels. The sound was visceral; it penetrated the body along the seam where the stomach joins the chest and plunged down through the abdomen and legs. It was as if the singers, on the charge of each leather-tipped stroke, recycled the sound from their lungs, through the amplifiers of their throats, back down into the earth.

The evocation of sacred power inside the concrete walls of a Bureau of Indian Affairs school at first was puzzling. The juxtaposition of the sacred and profane in Lakota life can be unsettling. Speaking haltingly into a microphone, her voice charged with emotion, Celene Not Help Him, granddaughter of Iron Hail (a.k.a. Dewey Beard, the best-known Wounded Knee survivor, who died in 1955), gave a gripping account of the massacre. Meanwhile, at the other end of the gym, several boys from Manderson with whom I had ridden up to Bridger in the yellow school bus clawed through a box of Patagonia windbreakers that someone had donated to the riders. Families crammed into the bleachers ate sandwiches and cold chicken out of bags and cardboard boxes and Igloo coolers. Infants tottered across the floor. Under the bleachers teenagers flirted and teased. Elders in folding chairs lined against the walls nodded off or looked up dreamily as the drummers pounded and sang. A husky dog with black paws and a bushy muzzle trotted across the floor wearing a baggy green sweater over its chest and forelegs.

The seen and unseen worlds are separated in Lakota consciousness by a permeable membrane. Their circular concept of time permits little distancing between present-day matters and past events. Charted in linear segments across a printed page, a hundred years is a long time. Recounted in the lush vocabulary of the Lakota language, with its absence of past and future tenses, historical fact is transformed into a kind of luminous, never-ending, revivifying *now*.

The lights finally dimmed around eleven, the hubbub gradually ebbed. Recumbent bodies sprawled across the gymnasium floor. In a corner by the bleachers the Manderson boys and I had parked ourselves in a tangle of saddles, bridles, bedrolls, and backpacks. Next to us, their pallets lined up in parallel rows, a contingent of Japanese Buddhists sipped tea from cylindrical bottles; as if on cue, like a ballet ensemble, they lay down and closed their eyes. The confusion from our corner lingered after the lights went out. No doubt invigorated by the drumming, the Manderson boys hissed like cats and clobbered one another with saddle blankets and rolled-up socks. I leaned wearily against my river bag and closed my eyes.

"Hey, Beezy!" one of the boys called. "Hold my feather, will you?"

"Sure."

"Put it on top of your pack. It's been blessed by a medicine man. Don't let it touch the ground."

"What happens if it does?" I said.

"You get the bad luck," he replied with a grin.

— 6 —

The next morning I hitched a ride to the village of Bridger in a beat-up air force van driven by a jolly Oglala woman named Jeanette. The van carried supplies for the next night's camp, as well as the personal gear of the Manderson boys. Jeanette had a round jowly face and a booming voice which she didn't hesitate to unleash upon the snarl of vehicles clogging the slick, rutted road leading to the corral. "Move it or lose it, you assholes!" she roared through the half-opened window.

"Oops," she giggled, pressing a plump finger against her lips. "I guess I oughta work on my manners."

The air was ferociously cold, the sky impacted with chunks of stony clouds. Snow fell in swirling gusts that stung exposed patches of skin. Trailers, vans, pickups, and cars snaked across a frozen field between the town and the banks of the Cheyenne River. Inside the roomy corral, riders swinging lariats between stiff fingers stumbled after skittish horses. With scores of people converging simultaneously, the horses became spooked. Even after they were saddled they continued to rear and prance. Riders who were bucked off jumped back on, only to be bucked off again.

I was unable to locate the man who was supposed to rent me a horse. Given the cold and confusion, the bitter wind that cut to the bone, the prospect of a painful day in the saddle, the fact that I didn't find him was probably fortunate. "You can stay with me," Jeanette said. "I need someone to help drive the van to tonight's campsite."

It took a couple of hours, but the horses were finally chased down and saddled, and by 10:30 that first morning the riders had formed a circle on a stretch of snowy ground next to a store on the road that led out of Bridger. Swaddled in blankets, muffled in parkas, quilted in down-filled jackets, their faces protected by scarves and ski masks, their eyes shielded by dark glasses and snow goggles, the riders sat stiffly in their saddles. In the center of the circle, clutching a leather parfleche, stood a spiritual leader in a fur cap and royal-blue ankle-length coat belted around the waist with a beaded sash. Next to him, their faces purple with discomfort, stood a half-dozen drummers. Also in the center, impressively erect on their horses, sat several of the leaders of the

Big Foot riders: Alex White Plume, Jim Garrett, Birgil Kills Straight, Arvol Looking Horse, and Ron McNeill. Clad in a flowing red capote, at ease on the back of a powerful black stallion, Arvol held the sacred hoop, from which dangled a clutch of eagle feathers.

As the spiritual leader prayed and the drummers pounded, Birgil Kills Straight detached himself from the nucleus and rode around the circle counting the riders. There were 129. The closer the party progressed to Wounded Knee, the bigger the number would become. That first morning men, women, children, Indians, Asians, and *wasicu* were all bundled in an eclectic assortment of clothing. Faces were swathed with scarves, ears bound with woolen flaps, and fingers tubed with gloves. Some wore capes made of animal skins, others wore olive green army-issue overcoats, still others were enveloped like artichokes in layers of blankets. Eagle feathers drooped from hats, coats, saddles, and bridles. Patiently they waited in the terrible cold for the spiritual leader to complete his prayers. Patiently they waited for the drummers to cease their pounding.

With everyone accounted for and the ceremonies concluded, the riders moved out in a wide, sweeping, clockwise motion around the stationary point of the spiritual leader and drummers. To the creak of stiff leather and the crunch of muffled hoofbeats, they kicked their horses into a stuttery trot. The sun glimmered through a rent in the saturnine sky. Dogs barked. Outside the dissolving circle, women draped with quilts began keening in excited voices. *"Heyupa! Heyupa! Heyupa! Heyupa!"* the leaders cried, rising up in their stirrups and shaking their staffs and lances. The cry reverberated the length of the uncoiling line. The women ululated shrilly. Icy breath scrolled out the horses' nostrils. Their hooves tossed chunks of dry snow into the air. Trailing behind the riders, high-stepping over steamy mounds of green turds, came the walkers, led by the Japanese, who were thumping prayer drums and chanting.

Jeanette rode with a friend in another vehicle and turned the blue van over to me, which I piloted in a caravan of vehicles along a succession of unpaved country roads parallel to the path the riders took that first day. Sitting in the passenger seat was

Jeanette's son, an amiable sixteen-year-old named Bernard. Over a winter coat, Bernard wore one of the Patagonia windbreakers that had been given away the night before. As we chugged through spacious country glazed with icy snow, Bernard discussed with statistical precision the passing merits of the NFL's leading quarterbacks. Early afternoon found the caravan parked on the side of a desolate road topping the spine of an exposed ridge overlooking the Cheyenne River valley. The ridge was treeless; a vicious wind rocked the van on its wheels. The morning clouds had vanished and the sun shone with brittle intensity. Bernard and I took advantage of the lull to dash through the cold to a cluster of hay bales in a nearby field. As we were hastily relieving ourselves, we heard shouts from the caravan. "Riders! The riders!" Back up on the road, braced against the wind, we watched a column of ant-like figures toil up the ridge from the river bottom.

A lone horseman, out front, partially obscured by swirling snow, came loping toward the caravan. Sheets of frost coated the horse's chest and forelegs. A blue ski mask veiled the rider's face; a pair of opaque goggles banded his eyes. From the broad crown of a black hat fluttered a solitary eagle feather. The rider wore a scarlet coat with blousy sleeves fashioned from a Pendleton blanket. The coat drooped over black buckskin chaps to the tops of a pair of black leather boots. Midway along the caravan he reined in and pulled the mask and goggles down to his chin. "We've lost a dozen horses already!" he called. It was Ron McNeill, point man for the riders, a Hunkpapa from the Standing Rock Reservation. "We had to ride hard to make up for the late start. The trailers are picking up the lame horses. We've got to get out of this wind. Some of our people are ready to drop!"

Moments later the main body of riders passed by, a grim tableau of benumbed figures soldered to the backs of their weary mounts. The wind was as brutal as an ax blade. At a funereal pace the riders plodded by, heads down, faces tucked into scarves and bandannas, collars pulled up, ear flaps yanked down, their bodies clenched against the cold. Patches of yellow ice knobbled the horses' flanks. Labored snorts popped from their gaping nostrils. Their liquid eyes were red-rimmed with fatigue. The riders had come fifteen miles; they had another fifteen yet to go. Those faces that weren't protected by masks or scarves bore expressions that looked as if they had been set in concrete. The words of encouragement we tried to offer died quickly on our lips.

A party of mothers, waving sweaters and blankets, left the warmth of their vehicles to chase on foot after their children. Slowly the line of riders fizzled to a posse of stragglers. A dull pain marbled the stragglers' eyes. Bringing up the rear, cloaked in a soiled white duster, a silk scarf binding his skull, came Percy White Plume, Alex's brother. It was Percy's job to account for each rider whose horse gave out or pulled up lame. His ruddy, mustachioed face was grim and unsmiling. While the stragglers made for the windbreak of the hay bales, Percy paused beside the cab of a pickup and gulped down a slug of hot coffee. He spoke Lakota to the Indians in the pickup. To the *wasicu* he didn't know, he offered no acknowledgment. His saddle creaked like the rusty coupling of a railroad car as he rode past the blue van.

The caravan of support vehicles reached camp, located on the spread of a friendly white rancher named Fred McDaniels, a couple of hours before sunset. There was plenty of work to do, and we all pitched in, starting fires, digging pits, erecting tents, hauling water, boiling coffee (cowboy coffee, the grounds roasted to a bilious soup then flavored with clumps of sweet grass). I helped Alex White Plume (whose horse had given out the first hour that morning) throw up a tipi; the entire process, from aligning the poles in a vertical cluster to wrapping the frame with canvas, took less than ten minutes. A battered school bus carrying a load of Canadian-based Russian emigres rattled up to Alex's tipi. Two men swaddled in bear pelts threw down a stack of poles from the roof, and within minutes the Russians had their own tipi planted sturdily in place. The sight of the two structures (soon to be joined by a third) was gladdening; by nightfall we had established a real camp—cozy, hospitable, inviting.

It was well after dark when the riders finally arrived. The weary horses commenced snorting while they were still some distance away. Between the trees bordering the property, illuminated by the headlamps of the support vehicles, we could see the ghostly silhouettes plodding at a turtle-like crawl along the road.

A short while later, around a popping fire in the middle of camp, the riders formed a circle. Inside the circle Wilmer Stampede, the spiritual leader who had prayed this morning, prayed again in a language that seemed to break apart, syllable by syllable, like chunks of overripe fruit. The sound of drumming and singing wailed through the frigid air. Over a smoky pit at the edge of camp a team of women boiled pots of coffee and buffalo soup. The smell of food to the ravenous riders must have been maddening; when it came time to eat, they and the walkers would be served first. The shadowy outline of the mounted figures, elongated by the light from the fire, took on eerie proportions. The breath from the fatigued horses coiled through the air in silken wreaths. Then the drumming ceased and the riders were dismissed. For a moment nobody moved; the silhouettes of the riders were like cutouts glued to a flickering backdrop. Then, with a crackle of leather, the circle broke up. There were sighs, groans, calls for assistance. One man, his joints racked with pain, fell to the ground when he tried to dismount and lay there without moving.

That night those of us without a tent, tipi, or car slept in Fred McDaniels' barn. The planks on the second floor were strewn with dry straw. Cubicles and pens divided the hard-packed floor downstairs. A woman with two young children burrowed under a buffalo blanket in a corner directly beneath a cluster of stiff bridles dipping from a crossbeam. A radio producer from Vienna fashioned a straw pallet inside a tiny pen on which we both placed our sleeping bags. The producer's name was Dirk. He was a shy, well-mannered fellow with a melodious German accent. He had an oval face, soft blue eyes, and a smile that rippled between his cheeks like a length of wet string. Unfortunately, he'd stepped off the airplane in Rapid City ill-prepared for the cold. He borrowed a coat here, a hat there, a pair of gloves from someone else. His shaving gear he toted in a plastic sack. I gave him a sweater, extra socks, and long underwear. The expression on his gentle face as he zipped himself into his sleeping bag was gloomy and distracted. Outside in the pitch-black South Dakota night the temperature plummeted to forty below.

"It never gets this cold in Vienna," he mumbled as he squeezed his microphone and tape recorder into the bag next to his body.

"This time of year a mass of ice air creeps down from the Arctic and hangs over the flatlands like a lid," I said, remembering the sundog I'd seen two days before.

Dirk squirmed and fidgeted. A melancholy sigh escaped his lips.

"You sure come a long way to freeze to death," I said, trying to sound funny.

A look of anguish clouded his blue eyes. He gazed up at the crossbeams bolstering the barn roof. I piled straw the length of his bag and packed it into place.

Dirk's voice was dreamy and reflective. "As a boy I pretended to be an Indian. I wore feathers to school and carried a rubber tomahawk. I read Karl May's novels and watched movies about Geronimo and the Apaches. Every day I rode a pony across the prairie and at night I slept in a tipi with a crackling fire . . ."

"And now here you are spending the night in a strange barn on the outskirts of real-live Indian territory in the grip of the worst winter in these parts in twenty years."

A wheeze escaped his mouth. "In Vienna we have coffee-houses where we go on winter evenings to eat cake and chocolate and read newspapers from all over the world." His voice sounded as if it came from under an overturned cup.

"Be nice to be there now, eh?"

Dirk didn't reply. One by one the lights snapped off in the barn. Riders, walkers, support people settled down to a diminishing chorus of groans, rustling bedrolls, and crackling straw. Wearing my boots, hat, and gloves—after heaping the bag with straw—I zipped myself into a snug cocoon, leaving a tiny hole to breathe through. For the rest of the night I snoozed fitfully in half-hour increments, waking to acknowledge the cold, the pleasant fact that I was still alive.

2

Those persons who complain that the Sioux would not give the troops a stand-up fight should have seen the field after that mixup. To the Sioux warrior, the white men were only a side-issue, a nuisance: it was seldom that he took enough interest in them to fight more than was necessary. But, say the old men, if you want a hard fight, a real scrap, pit Sioux against Sioux. Then the fur will fly.

—*Stanley Vestal,* Sitting Bull: Champion of the Sioux *(1932)*

He was an old man, cranky and irascible. Of late he had become an international celebrity after being featured as a star attraction in Buffalo Bill's Wild West Show, which had toured Europe and the Atlantic Seaboard in the 1880s. He was stubborn, intractable, unregenerate, and egotistic. He was also charismatic, generous, perceptive, and shrewdly intelligent. After the battle at Little Big Horn, he had led his northern branch of the Teton Lakota, the fierce Hunkpapa, into Grandmother's Land (Canada) for four years. Now he was back, settled comfortably on the Standing Rock Agency straddling the boundary between North and South Dakota, stoking the flames of a religious craze called the Ghost Dance that had swept the reservations. His name in his own language was *Tatanka Iyotake.* To most people he was better know as Sitting Bull.

The agent in charge of Standing Rock in the fall of 1890 was a contentious, outspoken man named James McLaughlin.

McLaughlin was forty-eight years old, a Canadian by birth, handsome, slimly built, with prematurely white hair, and a dapper white handlebar mustache. McLaughlin's opinion of Sitting Bull was cynical and dismissive. "Sitting Bull is a man of low cunning, devoid of a single manly principle in his nature or an honorable trait of character, but on the contrary is capable of instigating and inciting others . . . to do any amount of mischief," he wrote to the commissioner of Indian Affairs in the fall of 1890. McLaughlin's obsessive fear was that, in the furor caused by the Ghost Dance, Sitting Bull might jump the reservation and flee south with his band to link up with Oglala dancers at Pine Ridge. A cadre of dedicated worshippers led by Short Bull and Kicking Bear had sequestered themselves deep in the lunar wastes of the Badlands, vowing to fight to the bitter finish if the U.S. Cavalry tried to bring them in. Short Bull and Kicking Bear were minor leaders, good men with respectable followings, devoted to the old ways, though neither possessed any real political clout; operating in relative isolation from Stronghold Table, miles from Pine Ridge, they could be monitored from a distance by the cavalry. But if Sitting Bull joined them the stakes would alter considerably. The Hunkpapa chief added an imponderable dimension to any situation he was involved in. He was the best-known Indian in North America, probably the entire world. Photographs of his craggy face had been reproduced in magazines and newspapers and on the covers of pulp novels. Agent McLaughlin was convinced that he must not be allowed to leave Standing Rock to join up with anyone. Though by 1890 Sitting Bull's influence over his own people had waned, white authorities still regarded him as a powerful figure.

He was a big man, burly, with broad shoulders and a strong, fleshy face. Most white people believed he had engineered the entrapment and annihilation of Custer's command in 1876. In a vision a few days before the conflict, he had seen blue-clad bodies tumble from the sky, but he took no part in the actual fighting. His stubbornness in favor of the old ways had fixed him indelibly in the public consciousness. After fleeing to Canada in 1877, he vowed never to return; but an Indian's attachment to his native land is powerful and compelling. Weary of living in a foreign country, homesick for the coulees and woody draws along the Grand and Moreau Rivers, Sitting Bull returned with the band after four years of exile and settled into reservation life. Much had changed in Dakota territory. Systematic killing by professional hunters had reduced the buffalo to a few scattered herds. White settlers were staking claims on what once had been Indian territory. Cities and towns were rising with clamorous rapidity.

An era was limping to a close, and on its heels came the mythographers of popular culture, who began the task of transforming the raw material of historical fact into the palatable fancy of mass consumption. Dime novelists such as Ned Buntline and showmen such as Buffalo Bill Cody spun gauzy webs of appealing fiction around the lives and exploits of the white men who conquered the West and the red men who resisted that conquest. A figure as prominent as Sitting Bull could hardly escape being transformed into a kind of pop icon. People back east were eager to learn more about the brooding, phlegmatic Hunkpapa who had helped devise the attack on Custer's hapless command. Movies had not yet been invented, and it was primarily through the newspapers and dime novels that stereotyped renditions of real flesh-and-blood characters were disseminated to a mass audience.

In the summer of 1885 Sitting Bull went on tour with Bill Cody's Wild West Show for three months. The show played to audiences in more than forty cities in the United States and Canada. Sitting Bull's pay was $150 a week, plus two weeks' advance, a $125 bonus for signing on, and a percentage of the gross on all photographs and autographs he sold of himself. One reason he signed on was his infatuation with Annie Oakley, another star performer and crack shot, who Sitting Bull dubbed *Watanya Cicilia*, "Little Sure Shot." In the United States he was booed and hissed by audiences for his involvement in the Custer massacre, whereas in Canada he was cheered and applauded.

Though encouraged by Bill Cody, Sitting Bull never again went on the Wild West Tour. Too much was going on at the

Standing Rock Agency for him to stay away for any length of time. In 1888, and again the following summer, federal commissioners from Washington, D.C., journeyed to the reservation to try and entice the majority of eligible males into signing an agreement that would transfer huge amounts of land from Indian to white control; the enormous acreage guaranteed the Lakota by the 1868 Treaty was deliberately being siphoned off by official government skulduggery. The old chief's personal power was also being challenged, not just by Agent McLaughlin but by Hunkpapa who had converted to Christianity and adopted the white man's ways. Amidst this turmoil, Sitting Bull, indomitable as a rock, held firm. He argued with the commissioners attempting to bilk the Hunkpapa out of land that belonged legally to them. He invited ghost dancers to perform on his property. He refused to convert to the Christian faith and continued to invoke the spirit of *tunkashila* through the ceremony of the sacred pipe.

He also enjoyed a brief flirtation with a wealthy, glamorous widow in her mid-forties from New Jersey named Catherine Weldon. In 1889 Mrs. Weldon came out to the Standing Rock Agency to lend her support to Hunkpapa efforts to resist the federal commission's attempt to wrest their land away. Almost immediately she came under Sitting Bull's spell. Rumors flew thick and fast. Sitting Bull currently had two wives (by a total of nine wives in his lifetime, he had sired sixteen children); would the white woman consent to be added to the list? The local press waxed hyperbolic about the relationship. "She Loves Sitting Bull" trumpeted a headline in *The Bismarck (North Dakota) Tribune* on July 2, 1889, followed by the subhead, "A New Jersey Widow Falls Victim to Sitting Bull's Charms." While it's doubtful the two were intimate, unquestionably she supplied him with money and clothes. (She also gave him a gold charm in the shape of a bull.) By stroking the old man's ego, Mrs. Weldon incurred the wrath of Agent McLaughlin, who regarded her as an obnoxious East Coast do-gooder whose silly humanitarianism stood in the way of the inevitable transformation of the Lakota from nomadic warriors to yeoman farmers.

By early December 1890 it was evident that McLaughlin

had to do something about the obstinate chief. Sitting Bull had to be deposed, exiled, kidnapped, eliminated—anything this side of actual murder, though a murder of sorts is exactly what occurred on the morning of December 15 when Sitting Bull was apprehended by tribal police. McLaughlin had been the agent at the Standing Rock reservation for several years; he knew that grudges between rival Indians ran deep, that personal animosities festered for generations. He was understandably reluctant to send white troops to Sitting Bull's encampment for fear of the furor it would cause; but to dispatch a platoon of tribal police consisting of officers from other tribes and clans, several of whom had been embroiled in blood feuds with members of Sitting Bull's band, several of whom were roundly despised for their successful conversion to the white man's ways, was to invite disaster.

McLaughlin believed the Lakota were a conquered race, and like any subjugated people they had to knuckle under; and that meant giving up the peripatetic life, forsaking the tipi for square houses, accepting the true faith, and learning to converse in English. It also meant, and this most emphatically, no more ghost dancing. The Ghost Dance was inimical to progress; it deluded the Indians into thinking they could revive the days of the buffalo. When McLaughlin heard from his spies in mid-October of 1890 that Sitting Bull had vowed to fight and die for the new religion, he made up his mind that the old man must be removed from the Standing Rock premises. To the Commissioner of Indian Affairs on October 17 he declared, "Sitting Bull is a high priest and leading apostle of this latest Indian absurdity; in a word he is the chief mischief-maker at this agency, and if he were not here this craze, so general among the Sioux, would never have gotten a foothold . . . He is an Indian unworthy of notice except as a disaffected intriguer who grasps every opportunity to maintain his power and popularity. His is opposed to everything of an elevating nature and is the most vain, pompous, and untruthful Indian that I ever knew."

By December 1 the threat of a massive outbreak seemed imminent, and McLaughlin was under pressure from generals and politicians alike to cap the bottle of the messiah craze before the contents spilled over. The agent's patience had worn thin. He was tired of the furor, tired of the dancing, tired of Sitting Bull's intransigence; he was also fearful that the wily chief might sneak off with his band to the Pine Ridge Agency and link up with the ghost dancers there. If that happened, there would be real trouble.

When the agent heard that Bill Cody had been instructed by General Nelson A. Miles, commander of all federal troops in the Dakotas, to induce the old chief to leave the reservation, he vowed to stop it. Bearing a wagonload of gifts, nursing the effects of an all-night drinking bash with the officers at Fort Yates, Cody jolted down a rutted road toward Sitting Bull's enclave one morning in late November 1890. Miles wanted the truculent Indian removed from Standing Rock as well, and the man for the job, he believed, was Sitting Bull's old boss and popularizer, the man who had made the chief's name a household word in North America. Halfway to the Grand River, Cody's entourage was decoyed back to Fort Yates by an enterprising mixed-blood scout name Louis Primeau. At the fort, Agent McLaughlin handed Cody a note from President Benjamin Harrison cancelling his mission. The telegraph wires between Fort Yates and Washington, D.C., had been humming. McLaughlin, a political appointee to a lucrative position, was not without friends in high places. His missive pleading for Cody's withdrawal from the reservation had been read by the secretary of interior, the secretary of war, and forwarded up the line to the chief executive. The agent wanted Sitting Bull put away as much as anyone, but he wanted to cast the net himself and draw it tight. With Cody out of the way, he was free to exercise a strategy of his own.

Early on the morning of December 15, a platoon of forty-three Indian policemen cantered through the wooded bottomlands of the Grand River. "You must not let him escape under any circumstances," McLaughlin had ordered the three leaders: Bull Head, Shave Head, and Red Tomahawk. The police were dressed in coarse, ill-fitting blue uniforms and black slouch hats; their necks were wrapped with white mufflers so they could identify one another in the fuzzy winter light in the event trouble broke out. Pinned to the breasts of their jackets were the shiny badges indicating their authority as enforcers of the white man's law on the Standing Rock Agency. Several of the men belonged to other tribes of the Teton Sioux. Sitting Bull and his followers were Hunkpapa; for outsiders in military blue to ride into the heart of a Hunkpapa encampment and arrest their leader was not only bold, it was ill mannered and foolish. The police had fortified themselves at Bull Head's house the night before with whiskey supplied by the U.S. Army. A company of regulars under Captain E. G. Fetchet was poised in support a short distance from Sitting Bull's encampment.

A denouement of the darkest sort was about to occur on the stage of the Standing Rock Agency. Though popular among his own band, Sitting Bull's influence among the mass of Hunkpapa had diminished since his return from Canada in 1881. To some Indian progressives, he was an obstacle to be removed at any cost. Cleverly exploiting the situation, McLaughlin had exacerbated the jealousies between rival headmen, turning Gall and John Grass, two former cohorts, into outspoken critics of Sitting Bull. Isolated, ignored, his prestige dwindling, Sitting Bull was in danger of withering into an artifact, paralyzed by his obsession with the past, unable to provide leadership for the future. (But he could still prophesy, he could still exercise the old magic; in the summer of 1889 he predicted a severe drought for Standing Rock, which did not ease until June of the following year when rain finally fell.) Sergeant Bull Head, with his neat, prosperous farm located a few miles upriver, was considered the prototype of the new Indian. Coyotes screeled and owls hooted from the black branches as Bull Head led the troop through the wet trees at dawn. A mass of gloomy clouds muscled down to the treetops. Icy droplets spattered the riders' shoulders and hat brims.

The plan was to apprehend the chief as quickly as possible and whisk him away before his followers had a chance to organize any serious resistance. Two men were detailed to saddle the trick horse that Bill Cody had given the chief in appreciation for his contribution to the Wild West Show; as they crept around to the corral, the others dismounted and took up defensive positions in the clearing in front of Sitting Bull's log cabin. The leaders rapped loudly on the plank door; entering, they found the chief awake, lying naked under a blanket. Sergeant Bull Head explained the purpose of their mission. Sitting Bull appeared cooperative; with the help of his women, he began to dress. Hearing shouts and cries in the yard, Bull Head, Shave Head, and Red Tomahawk hurriedly tried to pull the rest of Sitting Bull's clothes over his hulking frame. "I will dress myself," the chief muttered. And then, perhaps with intended irony, he added, "You do not need to honor me this way."

Outside, alarmed followers of the old chief had gathered in an angry mob. It was nearly light; torches and kerosene lamps luridly illuminated the faces of the people in the yard. The press of hostile followers had stretched thin the police cordon blocking the way to the cabin. Inside, the three leaders wrestled Sitting Bull to the door. When Sitting Bull tried to brace himself against the frame, they kicked at his legs and hacked at his arms and thrust him out into the damp air. Cries of alarm greeted the chief's appearance. Suddenly a voice from somewhere drifted over the melee in a wailing plaint: "Sitting Bull, you have always been a brave man. What are you going to do now?" The effect on the old chief was cathartic. He stiffened and dug his heels into the ground. Bull Head and Shave Head had hold of his arms; Red Tomahawk stood directly behind him, clutching his neck and shoulders in a hammerlock. The voice was like a command which the old man could not resist. "Then I will not go," he declared in a voice loud enough for everyone to hear.

Catch-the-Bear, a loyal follower, threw off his blanket and marched toward Sitting Bull, levering a cartridge into the chamber of his Winchester. A feud of longstanding had simmered between Catch-the-Bear and Sergeant Bull Head; the sight of this detested adversary manhandling his leader brought the blood rushing to his eyes. Bull Head saw him coming, but before he could raise his own weapon, Catch-the-Bear fired. The slug caught Bull Head in the ribs; grimacing, he pivoted on one foot and fired a shot from his pistol directly into Sitting Bull's chest. The same instant Red Tomahawk, in the manner of a professional assassin, coolly blew out the back of the old man's skull with a point-blank shot. Sitting Bull collapsed lifeless to the ground like a bag of sand.

A vicious fight erupted at close quarters. Lone Tree, a relative of Bull Head's, sprang at Catch-the-Bear, wrenched the Winchester from his hands, clubbed him with the butt, and pumped a bullet into his body. Followers of Sitting Bull swarmed all over the police, shooting, clubbing, slashing with knives. The horse that Buffalo Bill had given to Sitting Bull and that had been saddled and led out from the corral knelt down in the yard as it had been trained to do under the command of a cracking whip and began punching the damp air with its hooves. Overwhelmed, the police retreated behind the cabin or back through the door, dragging their dead and wounded with them. Splinters exploded from the log walls as Sitting Bull's enraged followers opened fire with every gun they had. Inside the dingy cabin, under a pile of blankets, there was a suspicious movement; when the blankets were dragged away, Crow Foot, Sitting Bull's seventeen-year-old son, sat up, shivering. "My uncles," he pleaded, "don't kill me! I don't want to die!" Bull Head, lying on a pallet, blood seeping from the bullet wound in his abdomen, was in no mood to be charitable. "He is one of them that caused this trouble," he grunted. A blow to the face from Red Tomahawk sent the boy reeling through the cabin door. Outside in the bloody yard, a few feet from the corpse of his father, Crow Foot fell dead, punctured with bullets.

The fight ended as abruptly as it began. Alerted by the sound of gunfire, Captain Fetchet's company arrived on the run, set up a Hotchkiss gun, and dropped a couple of shells into the yard. Sitting Bull's followers melted into the trees. Fetchet's men entered the yard and began administering first aid to the survivors. Six tribal policemen eventually succumbed to their wounds. In the yard there were already eight dead Indians, including Crow Foot and Sitting Bull, and two dead horses. The women uttered a piercing shriek. One of the dead police was named John Strong Arm. When his relatives discovered the body, they added their lament to that of Sitting Bull's wives. A cousin of the slain man named Holy Medicine picked up a neck yoke from a pile of farm tools and marched over to Sitting Bull's corpse and bashed the dead man's face to a bloody, unrecognizable mess. "What the hell did you do that for?" a soldier cried, shoving him away with his rifle. A sergeant in charge of the detail, fearful that the body, awash in a mass of blood, might freeze to the ground, ordered a private to stand guard to prevent further mutilation.

3

On the south side of Rapid City, there is a long, high ridge. That is really a giant man lying there. At the east end of the ridge there is an outcropping of stone that is shaped very much like bare feet with toes. In the middle you can see the rounded form of a full stomach, and at the west end a head complete with its nose! In the early days, whenever medicine men came to Rapid City, they did not come by the easy flat way to the east; they climbed over that man because of his sacredness.

—*Fools Crow (1979)*

At sunrise the temperature was around twenty below. Inside the cavernous barn people woke reluctantly. In the tiny pen we had appropriated for ourselves, Dirk inched painfully out of the cocoon of his red sleeping bag. His round face was soiled with fatigue, his pale cheeks were fuzzy with the first hint of an apricot-colored beard.

"Good morning," I offered noncommittally.

Dirk stared at me glassy-eyed. Then, remembering where he was, he whispered, "Oh God," in an uneasy voice.

The camp came slowly alive. By eight o'clock most of the horses had been chased down and saddled and brought to the circle where Wilmer Stampede, impressive once again as he had been the first morning in an ankle-length great coat with a beaded waistband, offered a prayer to the thumping of a drum. The riders swung arthritically into their saddles; quietly, minus the hoopla and keening of the previous morning, the circle unraveled into a ragged line that played out onto the unpaved country road in front of the ranch house. Tapping prayer drums and chanting, the walkers followed in their wake. While the riders traveled overland across pastures and fields, the walkers stuck to the roads that inched across the level landscape at right angles. They were led by a Buddhist nun in her mid-forties named June-San. For the third consecutive year, June-San had come from her native Japan to retrace Big Foot's historic path. In 1988 she had walked by herself, hoofing overland in the wake of the riders; deep inside the Badlands one night she got lost and nearly perished of exposure. Because of the distances and nasty weather, the *Sitanka Wokiksuye* leaders had decided this year that the walkers would stick to the roads and be escorted by support vehicles.

Those of us left policed the camp as best we could, dismantling tents and tipis, dousing fires and packing up food; the crusty snow bore the imprint of hundreds of pairs of feet and countless bits of debris. The morning sky was filmy with tattered clouds; the temperature, warming up to ten below, was almost pleasant. To prevent the engine from icing up, Jeanette had run the blue van all night; along with Bernard and her other son, Antoine, she had slept in back on top of a pile of equipment. Her brother, Dale Looks Twice, slept there also. Dale was program director at KILI radio station on the Pine Ridge Reservation. KILI was broadcasting up-to-the-minute reports of the progress of the riders and walkers; Dale was along to monitor the situation and obtain interviews with participants which would air the next day. Like his sister, he had an earthy sense of humor. A compact man with wide shoulders and a mouth full of gaping teeth, he slid behind the wheel around ten that morning and guided the van away from the ranch carrying Bernard, Antoine, Dirk, and myself. Dirk was looking more cheerful after several cups of sugar-laced coffee.

Negotiating a series of right-angle turns in the company of other vehicles, we made our way in the general direction of the tourist town of Wall, home of the famous drugstore. Dale was congenial and funny, sharing stories about his life in a velvety baritone. His memories of the Catholic boarding schools on Pine Ridge were bitter and unpleasant. Whenever the boys were caught speaking Lakota, the priests whipped their hands with a leather belt. "Imagine that," Dale commented, puffing a cigarette and popping a fresh mint into his mouth. "We were beaten for speaking our own language."

We reached Wall and paused for gas and a bite to eat, then crossed Interstate 90, which bisects South Dakota in a nearly unwavering line from Sioux Falls on the eastern border to Rapid City in the west. Dale's face lost some of its introspective shadow. "I always feel better when I get south of the interstate. The Badlands are up ahead. Beyond that, home."

Midafternoon, under the scowl of a worsening sky, we pulled into camp, located on a flat expanse of tableland a few miles north of the Badlands Wall. The camp did not look promising; other than a weather-ravaged church with a cracked and peeling roof, there was no cover anywhere: no trees, no hills, no creeks or ravines to hunker down into. The land was as level as a basketball court; to the south and east it planed off into an infinity of gathering darkness. Where we would sleep tonight was anyone's guess. I'd brought a tent, a flimsy affair, which in this weather was useless. The van would be occupied by Dale, Jeanette, Antoine, and Bernard. This close to the reservation, many riders could go home and spend the night in their warm beds. But not us outsiders. We had to make do with whatever came along.

Upon inspection, Dirk and I found that the door to the church was securely padlocked; the pews had been removed and the interior was vacant. Dirk lit a cigarette and stared out at the forlorn landscape. The wind was picking up. Whirligigs of powdery snow pirouetted through the air.

"So what do you think's going to happen to us?" I asked.

"I think we're going to die," Dirk sighed. His blue eyes were cloudy with apprehension.

I helped a party of people dig a shallow pit out of the frozen earth for the cook fire. We took turns gouging the rigid soil with a pickax and spade; surprisingly, the earth broke up easier than expected. A tall, strapping fellow from Hamburg, Germany, named Axel Koester rotated with me on the pickax. The labor brought a film of sweat to our limbs and faces, which felt good at first then progressively more uncomfortable as the cold clamped down, freezing the sweat like a laminated veneer against our bodies. More cars and vans arrived at the campsite. The cook tent was erected, along with a tent where the fasters, both riders and walkers, would sleep the night.

The fasters occupied a unique niche in the pecking order of the *Sitanka Wokiksuye* participants. In honor of the ride, out of respect for the spirits of those who fell at Wounded Knee a century ago, they elected to go without food for the first three days. They were a hardy breed: Lakota, Japanese, *wasicu;* they were veterans of other vigils, other fasts, other pilgrimages all over the world. At night they were quarantined in their own wall-sided, green canvas tent, equipped with a portable wood-burning stove. Within minutes after being installed at the exposed campsite alongside the abandoned church, the stove was belching smoke out its thin metal stack.

Axel and I loaded the pit we had dug with split logs and brush; then we lowered the iron grill into place. Two slabs of buffalo ribs were unwrapped from a scroll of butcher's paper and broken up into bony chunks with an ax. "Buffalo soup," said an elderly Lakota woman with a face like a clay plate scored with countless lines. She tossed the chunks into a pot. "Just like the old days. You boys are gonna learn to live like Indians by the time we reach Wounded Knee."

As Axel and I labored with the pickax, a tall, thin, moody-looking fellow stood off to one side, leaning against the peeling boards of the church wall, observing our progress with a bemused grin. He didn't say anything; he made no effort to lend a hand; later I learned he was fasting and could barely muster the strength to stay on his feet. His name was George White Thunder. He was forty years old, an Oglala from Pine Ridge. His great-grandfather had been killed at Wounded Knee. George had started the journey from Bridger as a rider. The second day, beaten down by the cold, bleeding from the nostrils, his horse had given out. With no backup, George had to make his way to Wounded Knee as best he could. Like the others that first evening at the Takini School, he had touched the sacred hoop and taken the vow. An eagle feather pinned to the crown of his wool cap slanted awkwardly to his shoulder. Tomorrow he intended to join June-San and the walkers.

Under the stolid clumping of his features, George displayed an irrepressible humor. His life had been memorable. At thirteen he ran away from home. For years he hoboed around the country, working odd jobs, sleeping in cardboard boxes, brawling in taverns, cooling off in county jails. His face was like a relief map of the tumultuous journey. Deep lines creased his jowls and the corners of his eyes. His nose was a battered plug. When he smiled, his melancholy eyes ignited with enthusiasm. When he laughed, an infectious giggle sputtered between his lips.

After helping with the fire pit, I drifted around to the front of the padlocked church, peering into the windows, curious as to how cold it might be inside. The congregation door faced south. George was there, standing on the concrete steps, rolling a filter cigarette between his fingers as if it were a chicken bone. We fell into conversation. He spoke about his life, the hard times on the road. In 1986, at the time of the first Big Foot Memorial Ride, he quit carousing and returned to Pine Ridge. He participated in a Sun Dance, and the piercing helped restore his equilibrium. He didn't want to talk about the experience, and I didn't ask any questions. His moodiness masked an unknown range of emotions. He was open about some things, guarded about others. We stood in silence under the lid of a glum winter sky, watching people crawl out of their cars and vans and hobble urgently through the paralyzing cold to the shelter of the fire on the east side of the church. Then he told me about a scene he'd witnessed as a boy.

He was living with his grandparents on the Pine Ridge Reservation between Manderson and Porcupine. It was a hot summer afternoon; storm clouds were piling up in the west. "I was outside with my grandfather when suddenly it got dark, and my grandfather looked up and his face seemed to change. Something came over it, I don't know what, a funny look, but he wasn't scared. It's like he knew what was coming. He told me to go in the house with my grandmother. I hid by the bedroom window and peeked through the curtain."

George's voice was barely audible. The wind whipped

around the corners of the weathered church; tucked inside the steps, we were protected from the worst blasts.

"A ship of some kind shaped like an iron skillet came out of the dark sky over the yard and settled down with a whoosh. From a door a woman stepped out wearing a spotted calico dress like the one my grandmother wore. The woman was old and frail. She walked down the flight of steps holding on to a rail. Behind her was a tall man dressed in a black coat wearing a stovepipe hat like the pictures you see of Abraham Lincoln. He had a beard like Abe Lincoln's, too. In his hand he had a letter. He said something to my grandfather and handed him the letter. Then he went back into the ship. The woman in the calico dress didn't want to go back to the ship. She kept looking at the house and yard as if she'd seen them before. The man in the stovepipe hat said something to her. Reluctantly, like her shoes were full of sand, she walked back up the steps and disappeared. The ship rose off the ground and sailed west through the dark sky in the direction of the Black Hills."

George lit another Marlboro and stared hungrily at the filter. "My grandfather came into the house and told my grandmother to saddle his horse. He told me to help her. In his hand he held the letter, which looked like any other letter. There was even a stamp on it. I remember that. Something was written on the outside, but I was too little to know how to read. We got the horse saddled and brought it to the house. Meanwhile, more dark clouds had come up. We could hear thunder and see lightning. All around us it looked like it was raining, but not a drop fell on the house or yard. It stayed dry there as if a bowl had been tipped upside down over it.

"'Where are you going?' my grandmother said to my grandfather.

"'I'll be back in a while,' he said. 'I got to deliver this.' He said somebody's name but I didn't know it. My grandmother must have known the name 'cause she nodded like it was the right thing to do. She patted the horse and my grandfather rode off toward the west where there were more dark clouds and it looked like it was raining real hard."

George chuckled and finished the cigarette and ground it

out on the concrete steps. He cupped the filter in his palm and gazed at it wistfully as if it were a peanut or a piece of candy. The same husky dog I'd seen that first night in the Takini School gym, wearing the same baggy green sweater, trotted past the church steps with its head up and its muzzle twitching. The dog seemed to know where it was going. We watched it stride across the snow and disappear into the corral where several horses were already shivering. George fired up a fresh cigarette and bit down on the filter. His eyes were puffy slits; behind those slits the pupils were barely visible. "If they'd open this church up, we could spend the night on the floor out of the wind. We'd be okay then. They say it's bad luck to spend the night in an empty church. Too many ghosts. I know the white man who owns this property. He's a good man and he'd let us stay, but I can't force the lock without his permission. And he's in no shape to give anybody permission for anything. He's dying of cancer in a hospital in Denver."

"What happened to your grandfather?" I asked.

"He died, too. He died of cancer."

"No, no. I mean the letter. Did he deliver the letter to the right person?"

George squeezed his pulpy face into a thoughtful pout. "I think so. When he got back home that night, I heard him talking in the bedroom to my grandmother. But they were talking Lakota and I couldn't understand much. It sounded like they were talking the kind of language they used to talk way back when they could talk to animals. I asked him next morning if he had delivered the letter and he said 'Uh-huh.'"

"Uh-huh?"

"Like that. 'Uh-huh.' That was it. He never said anything more about it."

The husky dog reappeared at the edge of the corral and trotted toward the fire. The wind blasted over the roof of the church. We could hear the plank boards groaning against the foundation. In the angle formed by the junction of the concrete steps and the wooden wall there was a space big enough to wedge a body against, my body, enveloped in the sleeve of a down-filled bag, slumped into a fetal ball, within crawling distance of the fire.

I looked off at the snow-glazed flatland stretching in the direction of the Badlands Wall. The land seemed to go on and on, sweeping to an endless expanse. In a couple of hours it would be dark. The bitter cold and socked-in sky had pinched every bit of warmth and color from the air, leaving it dry and transparent, the tincture of cigarette ash, bleak and depressing.

"That's an interesting story, George," I remarked.

"I got others," he said reassuringly.

Night came early to the empty tableland. A night as dark as I could remember, an abysmal fold of encompassing blackness, with patches of pale stars glimmering between masses of drifting clouds. The temperature dropped; with the wind gusting in fits and starts, the cold was numbing. Around six the riders trooped in on a rumble of dull hooves and formed their circle; after the prayers they led their horses to the fenced-in yard, which already was provisioned with hay. Pots of coffee and buffalo soup frothed over the fire. The riders crowded around, dunking fry bread into soup bowls, swallowing ravenously. The ride had not been as strenuous as the one the day before. The weather was better, the distances shorter, the terrain consistently level. Only a few horses had pulled up lame or developed pneumonia.

Away from the yard and church (whose front door remained securely locked) cedar logs were stacked in a pile, and after supper a bonfire was ignited around which a crowd quickly gathered. Alex White Plume raised the talking stick and the crowd fell silent. It was the Lakota custom that whoever held the stick commanded attention for as long as he or she wanted. Alex issued words of welcome and reiterated the objectives of the Big Foot Memorial Ride. In contrast to his brother Percy, Alex's chin and upper lip were smooth; his long hair fell to his shoulders. A member of the Oglala Tribal council, an original *Sitanka Wokiksuye* rider and organizer, Alex had been highly visible for the past few days. He was personable and articulate, a natural leader, with a shy and engaging smile.

Arvol Looking Horse took the stick after Alex and spoke in halting tones, choosing his words carefully, letting the silences underscore the simplicity of what he had to say. He spoke

English tentatively, in simple straight-forward sentences. The pitted cheeks of his swarthy face glowed in the reflection of the bonfire flames. Arvol was selected by his grandmother at age twelve to be the future keeper of the sacred pipe for the entire Lakota nation; the responsibility brought with it a mandate to live an exemplary traditional life. The holiest of Lakota artifacts, the pipe, according to scientific tests, had been given to the people by White Buffalo Calf Woman at least four thousand years ago. The pipe was carefully wrapped and kept in its own place of concealment somewhere in the Cheyenne River Reservation, home of the Miniconjou, Big Foot's people. Only under special circumstances was it brought out to be viewed; the event of the unveiling was momentous, a time of solemn reconsecration to the principles of Lakota spiritual life.

Riders and walkers were braving the terrible cold, Arvol said as he gazed into the flames, so that the spirits of the ancestors could finally be released and the Lakota people could put the horror of Wounded Knee behind them and face the future with courage and hope. A chorus of guttural *"Haus!"* greeted his remarks. The fire crackled and flamed. Smoke belched up, stinging the eyes of those standing on the downwind side. The stick was passed to the next person and the next, and so on clockwise around the circle of shivering listeners. Indians from all over North America were present, Europeans from all over Europe— French, Italian, German, English, Dutch, Scandinavian, Czech. A Mexican from Chihuahua, his bowed legs wrapped in a pair of leather chaps, declared in broken English his heartfelt solidarity with dispossessed people of every race and nationality. A German from Düsseldorf said the Indian way of life, with its spiritual attitude toward the earth, offered the only hope of salvation for mankind. Several Indians delivered their remarks in Lakota. One or two expressed a lingering bitterness toward white people. These speeches were brief; Lakota courtesy precludes any sort of pointed or lengthy rudeness toward outsiders. The majority of Indians spoke fervently of reconciliation, of binding up the wounds, of a future where the old ways would be respected and observed.

The cold was appalling. The wind walloped down from the

north, stirring the fire, kicking up coils of acrid smoke. People coughed and sneezed and rubbed their smarting eyes and swatted at the fiery sparks that landed on their sleeves and legs and in their beards. The clouds had disappeared; a faint diadem of stars dimly illumined the brooding darkness. Face-on to the roaring fire, it was uncomfortably warm; within seconds after turning away, cheeks, toes, and fingertips became painfully stiff. Like chunks of beef on a rotisserie, people pivoted on their heels trying to maintain some kind of overall warmth.

A tall, hatless, solidly built man took the stick. Instead of standing in place, he tramped back and forth in front of the raging fire, oblivious of the smoke and dancing sparks. The man's voice was hard and uninflected; his words clapped against the freezing air like slabs of wood. He said the real meaning of reconciliation had to include a satisfactory resolution of the Black Hills problem. It was the first time this age-old thorny issue had been raised at the powwow, and it was greeted with a chorus of approving grunts. The hills belonged by right of the 1868 treaty to the Indian people, he said. The hills had been illegally stolen from them by the federal government in the wake of Custer's quest for gold in 1874. The man concluded his remarks by introducing himself. His name was Dennis Banks, and though he was of Ojibway blood, he had spent a lot of time among the Lakota.

Then an older man with a bulbous nose protruding from under the visor of a fur cap took hold of the stick. He looked gravely around the circle, sucked in a deep breath, and sang:"Jingle bells, jingle bells, jingle all the way . . ." Everyone around the fire, Indian and *wasicu*, erupted with laughter. And then I remembered: it was Christmas Eve. This was the first mention of the holiday that I had heard all day. When the laughter finally subsided, the man composed himself and spoke of the relatives he had lost a hundred years ago, how each generation of his family had kept the memory alive by telling the story over and over. "The world has never been told the truth," he declared. "The army kept it a secret all this time. What happened back then was an act of butchery, plain and simple. You don't have to be an Indian to understand this. If your heart is good, just by listening to what we have to say around this council fire, you will know we speak the truth. Would we be out here tonight in this cold if we did not believe that our ancestors had been murdered? We have homes. We have beds to sleep in. A few of us even have Christmas presents to open in the morning." Then he sang the words of another carol and everyone laughed and the man smiled, his full-lipped mouth bowing into an exaggerated grin. He signed off with the words, *"Mitakuye oyasin,* we are all related." A chorus of *"Haus!"* punctuated the air. As if on cue the wind pummeled the fire, igniting a flurry of sparks that hissed and spat through the downwind arc of the circle before swirling out in fiery tracers across the frozen snow.

It was late. Another hard day had come to a close. Rumor of a sanctuary in a schoolhouse in the nearby town of Interior rippled around the fire. The news relieved our worst anxieties as to where we would put our heads that night. Bob Keyes, a reporter from the *Sioux Falls (South Dakota) Argus-Leader,* volunteered to transport myself and two others to the school in his car. The powwow was still in progress as we got ready to leave; the talking stick had almost completed it circuit when a young Cree from Canada stepped forth. Holding the stick horizontally like a man balancing on a tight rope, the Cree expressed puzzlement over the fact that white people could actually have abandoned their homelands in Ireland, England, Germany, Hungary, and Italy to come to a land they knew nothing about and where they did not really belong. "That was your land," he said, "over there, in Europe. That land nurtured you and gave you wealth and strength. The bones of your ancestors are buried there. Their bones consecrate the land of your origin. How could you possibly abandon them? Now you live as orphans in a new land you do not understand and most likely never will. In your fear and insecurity you have fouled this land beyond repair. The spirits of your ancestors gave you wisdom and consolation. They kept you from ruining the land over there. By coming here, you cut yourself off from the source of your best wisdom. How could you turn away from the spirits who gave you everything? No wonder you have behaved so badly over here. No Indian would do that. No Indian would voluntarily abandon the bones of his ancestors. If he did, he would no longer call himself an Indian."

The gymnasium of the school in the little town of Interior was packed with people. Toting our gear, we threaded a path through a maze of pallets and bedrolls looking for a space in which to settle. The Manderson schoolboys had already parked themselves, and they called me over to bunk with them. They had ridden hard that day, and they had stories to tell of being cold and getting lost and not having enough to eat. Fred and Denny, Richard and Antoine, Bernard and Roy—they were all there, their blankets and saddles and sleeping bags occupying a messy pile at the edge of the basketball court. Despite their fatigue, they were full of enthusiasm and good cheer, all except Roy, the youngest. Roy was nine years old, a fourth grader. It was evident that the trip was beginning to wear on him. His face was pinched and thin; the color had drained from his cheeks. Despite the warmth inside the gym, he kept shivering and coughing. I gave him a chocolate bar, which he gulped in two bites. Then he pulled his bedroll next to mine and rested his head on my river bag. "He was crying earlier," said Fred Brown Bull, oldest of the boys, a tall, rangy sixteen-year-old. "We couldn't get him to quit. The cold is tough on these little guys."

Fred did calf roping and bronc riding in summer rodeos. His big hands were splotched with thorny calluses. This morning, at Fred McDaniels' ranch, I was holding the bit of the horse he had just mounted when the horse suddenly reared, throwing Fred off and sending me lurching away from the flailing hooves in panic. Fred landed in the snow with a thunk. There was loud laughter from those who witnessed the fall, hoots and catcalls; with the agility of an acrobat Fred leaped back on the horse, snatched hold of the reins, and settled the animal down. I knew at that moment that not meeting up with the man who was to rent me a horse was the best thing that could have happened. One day in the saddle in this merciless cold would reduce me to a mass of scrambled entrails and splintered bones.

It was after midnight when the gymnasium lights finally blinked out. The babble of conversation dwindled to a few groans and sleepy yawns. Scuffles flared up among the younger riders, then quickly died down. The air inside the gym was heavy with the fatigue of two days' travel. The communal feelings engendered by the powwow carried over into this warm place. People made room for one another on the floor. They shared food and bedding. They swapped clothes.

Roy burrowed under a woolly blanket and rubbed his shoulder like a cat against the bulge of my river bag. Before giving himself up to exhaustion, he reached out past my chin and patted the top of my head. "Goodnight, Beezy," he whispered.

"Goodnight, Roy."

I closed my eyes. My legs twitched. My joints ached. I tried shifting to a more comfortable position. Snores rose and fell in the muffled air. The feeling of relief, of being inside a protected place, was evident in the swelling volume of contented slumber that rose to the rafters. Outside, the wind slammed against the windows of the little school.

Sometime during the night Roy woke up crying. He blubbered a few times then succumbed to a rash of sobbing.

"Roy . . . hey, Roy. You'll be okay." I reached out and rubbed his shoulder and stroked his hair.

After a bit he calmed down. A hand came out from under the blanket and fumbled for the top of my head. "Beezy . . . hey, Beezy," he called.

"Yo, Roy . . . I'm here."

"G'night, Beezy."

"Goodnight, Roy."

I could feel his breath against my face, cool and slightly labored, which gradually subsided to a steady intake and exhalation. A collective sigh of weary contentment floated off the gymnasium floor. Somewhere, several hundred miles to the southeast, my own family was sleeping soundly, full of holiday cheer, pleased (no doubt) with the packages it was our custom to open on Christmas Eve. In my sleepless state, my memory went back. One holiday season in my hometown of St. Joseph, Missouri, downtown with my older brother doing some last-minute shopping, we ran into a high-school classmate of his, an Indian boy named Jim Rhodd. Jim came from northeast Kansas, from the tiny Iowa Indian Reservation located near White Cloud, on the Missouri River. He attended high school in St. Joseph, the biggest river town between Omaha and Kansas City. In those less racially sensitive days, Jim's nickname was "Chief." Everyone called him that, including my brother. It was not a title of disparagement; in reality, Jim was a bonafide chief of the Iowa band, having been elevated to the position by his grandfather at the age of sixteen. The event had brought photographers from *Life Magazine* all the way out from New York. The article had transformed Jim into a local celebrity.

The time was the early 1950s. The weather was mild that particular afternoon, as it frequently is in western Missouri during Christmastime. I was wrapped in a winter coat. Jim and my brother, with typical adolescent bravado, wore as an outer wrap only their high-school letter sweaters. The sweaters were white, they were woven of wool, and they flashed a special signal that the wearer was a jock, and a varsity jock at that. The chest and sleeves were decorated with letters and shiny medallions like campaign ribbons indicating meritorious service in a variety of sports. Jim's sweater was encrusted with emblems; a talented athlete, he was more versatile than my brother, who had earned letters only in football and baseball.

That afternoon Jim was dressed almost identical to my brother: Levis, penny loafers, Oxford button-down shirt. His luxurious black hair was clipped in the severe flattop style of the time. The only thing recognizably Indian about Jim was his face. In a Missouri high school not yet integrated by the 1954 Supreme Court decision, Jim Rhodd, on the strength of his ruddy full-blood face, stood out as different, separate, distinct. His face was full and fleshy, the features prominent and aloof, the eyes half-slotted behind high cheekbones. I couldn't take my eyes off his face. I was thirteen years old, and I had never seen a face like his before. I tried not to be rude. I looked away for a while at the wizened white woman in an ill-fitting Santa Claus costume standing nearby shaking a bell next to a tripod from which dangled a Salvation Army bucket half-filled with nickels and dimes, but not for long; as if attracted by a magnet, my eyes were pulled back to Jim Rhodd's exotic face. It was the oldest face I had ever seen—older, in some respects, than my grandmother's rotund German face. The skin was the color of the Missouri River on summer afternoons when the sun struck it at a certain angle: opaque and darkly textured, stippled with tiny pockmarks, crinkled with fluid lines; an ancient face, mysterious and suggestive. He talked a lot like my brother; they were built along the same stocky, broad-shouldered lines. They laughed at the same jokes, though behind the facade of socialization, in the fullness of his blood-tinted skin, the depth of otherness his dark eyes hauntingly conveyed, a gulf loomed between them that no amount of varsity games or sock hops could possibly bridge. After high school my brother would attend college, and after college he had a family business to come home to. Jim might go to Omaha or Kansas City for awhile, but eventually he would return to the Iowa reservation and be a chief to his people. A chief of what? I wondered. What did it mean to be an Indian chief in 1953? What did it mean to be an authentic, hereditary chief like Jimmy White Cloud Rhodd, with an ancestral identity light years removed from the penny loafer, Levi-clad mirror image he presented to my Anglo-German brother? Back then, Indians everywhere were under terrific pressure to conform to the dominant white culture. The 1950s was not a good time to be an Indian. In 1953 the Eisenhower Administration instigated a policy of assimilation that promoted the relocation of native people to urban settings, plus the termination of the special relationship between the federal government and those tribes it had signed treaties with in the nineteenth century. No wonder full bloods such as Jim Rhodd were walking anomalies, with their crewcuts, snappy shoes, and trendy shirts. Who were they? To what world did they belong? How did they view themselves in a society that regarded them as vestiges from another world, to be photographed in traditional regalia by popular magazines, to be befriended by contemporaries who could never really comprehend their special identity?

Sometime in the middle of the night Roy woke up crying again, and I reached out and tried to comfort him. I stroked his hair and touched his cheek, and after awhile he calmed down, and his breathing leveled out and the tears that wet my fingers ceased to flow. I think I'd been dreaming about Jim Rhodd, about the Missouri River, alongside of which we both had grown up. The river wound northwest from St. Joseph, swinging like a lariat between steep-sided bluffs, trenching a meander of liquid arcs all the way up through the Dakotas, where Roy's people once chased buffalo and hung from bone pegs in the hot sun and consulted the patterns of stars.

Roy's hand found mine. We squeezed each other's fingers till we both fell asleep.

4

When you return home you must make the dance, and all of you do it the same way. Dance for five days and one night. Then everybody should take a bath in the river and go home.

Be a good behave [sic] always. It will give a satisfaction in your life.

Do not tell no white man about this, but Jueses [sic] is now on the earth like a cloud. Everybody who was dead is alive again. I don't know when they will come here—this fall or in the spring. Then everybody will never be sick anymore and all will return to being young again.

Work for the white man, and do not make any trouble with them until you leave them.

Do not tell lie.

—Wovoka (Jack Wilson), from a letter written to the delegates of all the tribes who had come to hear his story in Nevada (1890)

The fight on the morning of December 15 was brief and nasty. By the time Captain Fetchet's troop had dispersed the old chief's cohorts along the Grand River, fourteen Indians lay dead or dying on the hard-packed ground. With the area secured and the wounded being tended to, the troopers lit fires and brewed coffee. Suddenly from the trees by the river burst a Hunkpapa warrior mounted on a black horse and wearing a ghost shirt decorated with animal emblems. This was Black Woman, a fervent dancer and champion of the old ways. Three times he charged through the line of startled bluecoats, shaking a feathered lance and singing at the top of his lungs. The Indian police opened fire, but the bullets zipped harmlessly into the woods. At the third charge, the warrior dashed between two troopers who volleyed several rounds but failed to bring him down. At the trees Black Woman reined in his mount. "Father," he wailed, "I thought you said you were going to live . . ." More bullets pattered against the bare branches. Members of Sitting Bull's band, watching from the bluffs, took note of the fact that the ghost-shirted warrior escaped unscathed.

Sitting Bull's mutilated body was loaded with the others into the wagon, and, with the wounded sitting or lying on the grisly cargo, the procession started for Fort Yates under military escort. The next day a carpenter named J. F. Waggoner made a coffin for Sitting Bull. The box measured two feet by two feet by six feet four inches. Sitting Bull was a big man, and he filled every inch of the space. As Waggoner worked, soldiers drifted in and asked to drive a nail into the coffin. When the box was finished, the body, with the face hideously disfigured, was placed inside wrapped in a blanket, frozen stiff, matted with dried blood, and perforated with seven bullet wounds. The box was then loaded on a two-wheeled cart and hauled by an old army mule to the post cemetery. Before the body was interred, Waggoner lifted the lid and poured five gallons of lime chloride into the box, along with a jug of muriatic acid. The lid was then nailed down and the coffin lowered. As clods from the shovel rattled down on the lid, fumes leaked between the boards in a mephitic vapor, causing the onlookers to gasp and turn away.

Rumors festered like weeds in the wake of the old man's death. The *Bismarck (North Dakota) Daily Tribune* ran a story declaring that the body in fact had been dismembered and the parts auctioned off to the highest bidders. (Relics of Indian remains were a big money draw in *wasicu* museums during the nineteenth century.) While no proof of this was ever discovered, drenching the body in quicklime brought dishonor to the Fort Yates' officials, both Indian and white. Was it to conceal the mutilation, to prevent his followers from obtaining the remains, or simply to show their contempt? Whatever, McLaughlin and his Hunkpapa allies were criticized by newspapers around the nation. The *Chicago Tribune* spoke of "the assassination of Sitting Bull." The *New York Herald* said, "There was, cruel as it may seem, a complete understanding from the Commanding Officer [McLaughlin] to the Indian Police that the slightest attempt to rescue the old medicine man should be a signal to send Sitting Bull to the happy hunting ground." The subsequent looting of Sitting Bull's compound by tribal police brought additional dishonor; a number of artifacts were turned over to Agent McLaughlin, who exhibited them for profit at the 1893 Columbus Exposition in Chicago.

General Nelson A. Miles, commander of military forces in the Dakotas, was furious when he heard about Sitting Bull's death. The fear and paranoia that the Ghost Dance had already incited among white settlers was bound to be aggravated by reaction of the Indians to the murder of their best-known leader. The last thing Miles wanted was bands of vengeful warriors roaming the countryside. He was particularly concerned about a group of Miniconjous under the leadership of a man named Big Foot. Big Foot's band was camped along the Cheyenne River, forty miles southwest of the spot where Sitting Bull had been slain. The band included ghost dancers and veterans of the Little Big Horn. Though Big Foot had participated in the battle, in the years since he had earned a well-deserved reputation as a diplomat and a conciliator; over the next few days those skills would be sorely tested. One contingent of his band agitated on behalf of joining the ghost dancers led by Short Bull and Kicking Bear on Stronghold Table deep in the Badlands. Another contingent wanted to stay where they were under the watchful eye of Colonel E. V. Sumner; in return for their compliance, Colonel Sumner promised to guarantee that their portion of rations was properly distributed during the cold months ahead.

A year before the catastrophe at Wounded Knee, a delegation of Indians had journeyed to Nevada to interview a Paiute shaman named Wovoka. (The man's Christian name was Jack Wilson.) From Wovoka they learned details of the Ghost Dance. Essentially the dance was a ritual that emphasized peace and nonviolence. "Do not fight . . . you must not fight," Wovoka told the tribesmen—Lakota, Cheyenne, Arapaho, Bannock, Crow—who traveled long distances to listen to the account of the vision that had befallen him. One day, out chopping wood, the Prophet (as he was known) was felled by a crack of thunder and transported by God up to Heaven. Heaven was a green and gentle land, well watered and arable, populated with wild animals, where people played and danced all day and never grew old. Heaven was also a place where the white man and his cultivated fields and noisy machinery and ugly cities were buried under an avalanche of fresh grass. The Prophet told his visitors that they could make this vision come true, provided they lived in peace and provided they performed a sacred ritual known as the Dance of the Souls Departed, or the Ghost Dance. The dance—a variation of the Paiute Round Dance, in which men and women formed a circle, held hands, and side-stepped to the left around a sacred tree or pole—for the lucky participants, resulted in just such a vision as the Prophet had described. After falling into a swoon, the dancers reported having seen their relatives alive and healthy, and more buffalo than they could possibly count.

Ecstatic visions were commonplace in nineteenth-century North America. Shakers, Quakers, Methodists, Baptists, and Adventists were but a few of the sects whose revival meetings frequently metamorphosed into bacchanals of body-quivering testimonials to God's infectious spirit. During the Great Awakening in the Mississippi and Ohio River valleys in the 1840s, Methodist circuit riders stirred their largely illiterate congregations to feverish pitches with their descriptions of the Kingdom of God settling like a celestial airship, festooned with crystal towers and paved with solid gold streets, upon the humid, malarial, mosquito-infested canebrakes and forests. Eyewitnesses offered graphic accounts of the physical convulsions that seized worshippers at the height of their ecstasy. An English traveler named J. Remy divided the convulsions into three categories: the rolls, the jerks, the barks. "The rolling exercise was affected by doubling themselves up, then rolling from one side to the other like a hoop," he described in a book entitled *A Journey to Great Salt Lake City* (1861). "The jerk consisted of violent spasms and twistings of every part of the body. Sometimes the head was twisted round so that the head was turned to the back, and the countenance so much distorted that not one of its features was to be recognized. When attacked by the jerks, they sometimes hopped like frogs, and the face and limbs underwent the most hideous contortions. The bark consisted of throwing themselves on all fours, growling, showing their teeth, and barking like dogs."

White people might shimmy and gyrate, they might gnash their teeth and roll their eyes, they might even twitch in the throes of convulsive shudders, but the specter of Indians dancing, even in a monotonous shuffle around a circle, was interpreted as a prelude to war. In the fall of 1890, newspapers around the nation sounded tocsins of alarm. "Great excitement at the Pine Ridge Agency," blared the *Chicago Tribune* on November 20: "Indians Dancing with Guns." "The Red Skins are Dancing the Dreaded Ghost Dance," boomed the *Omaha Daily Bee*.

The condition of the Lakota at the close of the 1880s was grim. The majority had been living on reservation land since 1877. In 1886 a huge tract of contiguous territory, on which they had hunted for generations, was carved up into six separate reservations. A year later, Senator Henry Dawes of Massachusetts, eager to divest the Lakota of more land under the aegis of bringing them closer to civilization, attached his name to a legislative act that further subdivided the Indians' ancestral holdings by allotting each family a parcel of 160 acres, which the families were expected to farm in a manner that would make them self-sufficient. The surplus land was auctioned off to white homesteaders for as little as fifty cents an acre, which further eroded their dwindling land base. During the 1880s a devastating drought, accompanied by grasshopper plagues, ravaged the Northern Plains, making farming, always a marginal occupation in that part of South Dakota, an almost impossible task. Federal budget constraints in 1889 forced Congress to cut back rations to the tribes; some legislators felt the belt-tightening would inspire the Indians to become more "productive." To complicate matters, food shipments were siphoned off by greedy middlemen; the problem was compounded by a sloppily conducted census of reservation populations, which reported fewer Indians than was actually the case.

Meanwhile, Christian missionaries had arrived in force. Protestant and Catholic proselytizers fanned out in search of converts, dividing the reservations between them like so many wedges of the ecclesiastical pie. The Sun Dance was officially banned; the *hanblechya* (vision quest) was discouraged; other rituals went underground in order to survive. Children were rounded up by tribal police and forced to attend church-supervised schools. Their hair was cut; they were outfitted in coarse shirts and wool trousers and sack-like dresses; they were chastised for speaking their own language. No wonder a dance that generated such pleasant memories of the old ways became so popular among them. (Though not with the majority of the population; at the height of the furor, in the summer of 1890, no more than a third of the entire Teton Sioux population was caught up in the fervor.)

Given time, the dance probably would have died out of its own insufficiencies. Though he permitted dancing in his own camp, Sitting Bull never became an adherent. Perhaps he was too much of a realist. He'd been all over the United States and Canada with Buffalo Bill's Wild West Show. He knew the size of the Atlantic seaboard cities; he'd seen the throngs of immigrants in the streets. Any effort to preserve the integrity of the old life would take more than a utopian vision to succeed; it would take a concerted strategy, high-tech weapons, warriors the caliber of Hump, Gall, and Crazy Horse, and they were either dead or resigned to the passivity of reservation life.

The Ghost Dance and the vision it inspired reflected the influence that white civilization had already made on Indian culture. The concept of a messiah, sent directly by God to instruct the people on how to redeem their lives; the imposition of a Kingdom of (Buffalo) Heaven on the face of the ravaged earth; the revivalist vigor of communal dancing far from the prying eyes of authority—these were products of the cross-fertilization of religious influences that already had made significant inroads into traditional Lakota beliefs. Thirteen years of reservation life had accelerated the process of transformation that eventually would bring the Lakota to the brink of cultural oblivion. Part Indian, part Christian, the Ghost Dance was a hybrid, the brainchild of a lonely Paiute farmhand in far-off Nevada, who wore

— 44 —

ranchers' clothes and a white felt hat, who believed in the Bible and regularly attended church—a man who today might be scornfully dismissed by traditionalists as an "apple" (red on the outside, white on the inside).

The dance bore no resemblance to a war dance. Women, children, elders took part. No weapons were included. The content of the songs emphasized reunification with the spirits of the dead. Deerskin was difficult to obtain, and the ghost shirts were fashioned primarily out of white cloth. Animal designs were painted on the fabric; the shirts were then passed through the purifying smoke of a prairie grass fire. *Wasicu* trappings such as silver or beaded jewelry were frowned upon; grouped in a circle around a sacred tree or pole, the dancers linked fingers and commenced a slow, shuffling drag-step around a circle, singing, praying, chanting, until seized by a vision, whereupon they fell into the dust.

Mrs. Z. A. Parker, a teacher on the Pine Ridge Reservation, observed a dance on June 20, 1890, along White Clay Creek. The sick and infirm were herded into the center of the circle. By joining the dance and losing consciousness, it was believed they would be cured. To a monotonous tune, the dancers chanted the words:

> Father, I come
> Mother, I come
> Brother, I come
> Father, give us back our arrows.

The words were repeated again and again until one by one, overwhelmed with a vision, the dancers staggered away from the ring and collapsed. "One woman fell a few feet from me," recounts Mrs. Parker. "She came toward us, her hair flying over her face, which was purple, looking as if the blood would burst through; her hands and arms moving wildly; every breath a pant and a groan; and she fell on her back, and went down like a log. I stepped up to her as she lay there motionless, but with every muscle twitching and quivering. She seemed to be perfectly unconscious. Some of the men and a few of the women would run, stepping high and pawing the air in a frightful manner. Some told me afterwards that they had a sensation as if the ground were rising toward them and would strike them in the face. Others would drop where they stood. One woman fell directly into the ring, and her husband stepped out and stood over her to prevent them from trampling upon her. No one ever disturbed those who fell or took any notice of them except to keep the crowd away."

The dance craze engendered a host of curious spin-offs. Quacks and charlatans, attracted to the charged atmosphere on the reservations, tried to peddle their own brand of evangelicalism to the confused Indians. On December 22, 1890, Pine Ridge tribal police picked up a white man wandering through the camps near White Clay Creek with a blanket draped around his shoulders. The name the man gave to agent Daniel Royer was A. C. Hopkins. He claimed to be from Iowa. For several weeks, traveling alone, he'd been trying to convince the Oglala that he was the messiah prophesied by Wovoka. The Indians weren't fooled; though Hopkins spoke no Lakota, the Oglala treated him with the respect they usually accorded the insane. When questioned by Agent Royer, Hopkins declared, "I claim to be Christ, the Messiah, in a poetic sense. The same poetic sense in which Hiawatha, Socrates, and General Grant are considered and esteemed the world over."

Agent Royer could barely contain his incredulity. "Prove that you are Christ," he demanded.

"Give me more time among these Indians and I will," Hopkins said stubbornly.

"I'll give you exactly one hour to get out of town," the humorless Royer snapped in response.

On the morning of December 18, survivors of the Sitting Bull slaying stumbled into Big Foot's camp on the Cheyenne River. News of the old chief's death electrified the Miniconjous, who numbered around 350 men, women, and children. Big Foot was in a quandary. His skills as a negotiator were considerable; Red Cloud and the other Pine Ridge leaders wanted him to come south and mediate between their pro– and anti–Ghost Dance factions. A hundred horses were offered as an inducement. Big Foot's own band was deeply divided on the subject of the dance. An influential medicine man who may or may not have been known as Yellow Bird (and from whom we shall hear again, but whose exact identity remains uncertain) agitated vigorously on behalf of the dance. Yellow Bird wore a typical ghost shirt with a V-neck, fringed with buckskin along the sleeves and hem, and decorated with animal and celestial fetishes. To placate this restless faction, Big Foot encouraged them to acquire fresh ammunition for the few Winchesters they possessed, to be used strictly in defense should the bluecoats attempt to break up their dancing. To the nondancers, Big Foot counseled patience and restraint. Up to this point, the chief's brand of passive diplomacy had worked; news of Sitting Bull's death and the arrival of at least twenty angry and embittered Hunkpapas now threatened to shatter that delicate equilibrium.

A troop of cavalry under Colonel E. V. Sumner was camped several miles downstream from Big Foot's band. Sumner had met earlier with the chief and was genuinely fond of him; when he received an order on December 19 from General Miles to apprehend Big Foot and escort his entire band to Fort Meade on the edge of the Black Hills, he hesitated. The wording of the order was ambiguous; after another meeting with Big Foot, Sumner felt confident the Miniconjou leader would not do anything rash. Sumner was disturbed, however, by the presence of the Hunkpapas among the band, and he urged Big Foot to cast them out, which, given their pitiable condition, Big Foot was reluctant to do. So, while Colonel Sumner dallied, the Hunkpapas spread their tale of Sitting Bull's treacherous death, and the Ghost Dance faction strengthened its resolve not to give up anything to the bluecoats. In the meantime, Big Foot caught a bug from a bout of influenza making the rounds through camp and found himself shivering with a high fever.

In response to a second order from General Miles on the twenty-second, Colonel Sumner woke up to the fact that, for the good of his career, he'd better make a move. Earlier, he had sent a courier to Big Foot requesting that the chief prepare his people for the long march to Fort Meade. When Big Foot failed to show up at his camp on the twenty-second, Sumner became concerned. He sent a local rancher named John Dunn, known to the Indians as Red Beard, to tell the Miniconjous to get a move on. Red Beard spoke fluent Lakota. The exact text of the message he delivered will never be known, but something evidently became scrambled in the transmission from Colonel Sumner through him to the Miniconjous. Instead of a simple order to pack their belongings and get ready to march to Fort Meade, the message, according to the Indians, contained an overt threat. They claimed that Dunn told them that the bluecoats were planning to surround the Miniconjou encampment at night and take everyone prisoner and shoot those who resisted. The leaders would then be placed in shackles and sent by train to an island in the eastern sea (Atlantic), where they were to be imprisoned in an old brick dungeon.

Whatever the gist of Red Beard's message, the effect on the Miniconjous was catalytic. Despite his friendliness toward the Lakota, Red Beard's military mission quite possibly was motivated by personal interest. The previous September, at the height of the Ghost Dance craze, he signed a petition with other *wasicu* ranchers requesting military protection should the Indians go on the warpath. A sizeable herd of cattle owned by Red Beard grazed on land a few miles from Big Foot's encampment.

No one knows for sure what Red Beard said to Big Foot during that fateful meeting. The order given to him by Colonel Sumner was not written down; Red Beard later claimed he told the Miniconjous exactly what he had been instructed to say by the officer. In the inquiry that followed the massacre, both Sumner and Red Beard were questioned by army investigators. Sumner's version of the event did not differ from Red Beard's. The army accepted their account, and the case was closed.

The shock of the news delivered by Red Beard rippled through Big Foot's camp. No sooner had the rancher ridden away than a council was called. Several headmen wanted to start immediately for Pine Ridge; others wanted to establish a defensive position at a nearby creek and wait and see what the bluecoats did. Big Foot counseled moving the entire band to Fort Bennett, on the Missouri River, where they would be safe and assured of receiving their winter rations. Advocates of the middle position won out; the camp was knocked down, horses saddled, and in an amazingly short time the Miniconjous were toiling up a long hogback out of the steep Cheyenne River valley to the defensive security of Deep Creek. At the top of the hogback—near the spot where, on the first day a hundred years later, the freezing *Sitanka Wokiksuye* riders had taken refuge from the biting cold behind hay bales—scouts reported a detachment of Colonel Sumner's men within five miles of the Miniconjou party. Another council was assembled. It appeared as if Red Beard was correct; the bluecoats were coming to take their leaders away to prison. (Actually the detachment was a patrol sent out by Colonel Sumner to find out where Big Foot's band had gone.) The decision was made to start for the sanctuary of Pine Ridge. Coughing, wheezing, Big Foot, his physical condition gradually deteriorating, gave his consent. The Indians headed south to safety.

5

Perhaps a wandering people is naturally difficult to convert.

—*Mari Sandoz,* Love Song to the Plains *(1961)*

Around six the lights stuttered on inside the gymnasium. Sprawled on pads and bedrolls across the hardwood floor, the sleepers stirred grumpily. The Manderson boys, especially Roy, hunched into fetal balls and shielded their eyes from the glare. Fred Brown Bull went from boy to boy, shaking them hard, thwacking the soles of their bare feet with a leather bridle. The younger boys moaned and protested, but Fred was relentless. Groggy, their faces pasty with fatigue, the boys rose sullenly to their feet.

Close by in the crowded gym a tall, robust, middle-aged man, twin queues of braided hair dangling over each shoulder, got to his feet with a slow, unhurried motion. The man was powerfully built, with a cylindrical chest and a fleshy overripe face. "Santa Claus is a racist!" he boomed in a hearty voice. "He didn't leave any presents for us 'skins!'" A few snickers greeted the remark, a few guffaws. But it was too early for witticisms, even those delivered by Russell Means, controversial American Indian Movement (AIM) leader. Russell chuckled at his own joke, smiled broadly, turning from right to left like a performer in front of a sympathetic audience; then he pulled a black leather vest over a plaid wool shirt and finished dressing.

At the campsite on the empty tableland the embers from the powwow fire gave off a stringy thread of smoke. In the dawning light the clapboard walls of the abandoned church looked as if they had dwindled in size during the night under the weight of the relentless cold. Riders and walkers gathered around the popping cook fire next to the east wall of the church to sip tepid coffee and puff cigarettes; coils of acrid smoke plumed through the grill, stinging everyone's eyes. One by one the fasters stumbled out of their tent. I recognized George White Thunder. He yawned and stretched his long arms over his head. Swaddled in a quilted blue jacket, his body seemed to have diminished during the night to a cluster of brittle sticks. Lipping a cigarette with hungry enthusiasm, he stepped to the fire and inhaled a snootful of biting smoke, which he relieved by wiping his nose on his sleeve.

Buckets of fresh water from a pump down the road were brought to the cooks, who replenished the tubs and soot-blackened pots gurgling on the grill. The faint odor of charred clothing and animal fur filtered through the scent of woodsmoke. "Gonna be a cold one," someone remarked, glancing up at the colorless sky. The remark went unchallenged. The cold was a given, an implacable reality; there was no evading or finessing its presence. The people around the fire pulled their hat brims down low and jacked up their scarves and collars; they drank more coffee and smoked more cigarettes and focused on whatever warm spark flickered inside their imaginations. The day would be numbing and arduous. The riders would be racked to the bone, and the walkers weary and footsore. Calls and shouts rang through the brightening air. In the corral the horses began to snort and blow and stamp their stiff hooves against the drum-tight earth. More riders arrived from wherever they had spent the night.

Two hours later, at the edge of the Badlands Wall, I watched the riders negotiate a tricky descent of Big Foot Pass. The pass was a major landmark on the memorial ride. Located within the boundaries of Badlands National Park, the pass tips precipitously down a runnelled wash of eroded flanks and ridges to the wide plain of the White River valley. A hundred years ago, after trekking across empty tableland, Big Foot's cavalcade of wagons and mounted warriors had paused at the rim of this impressive drop. Scouts reconnoitered a path down through the jumble of turtle-backed humps of betonite clay. The path was icy, patched with snow, bounded by sheer sides that fell away into steep ravines. By rope the wagons were guided down the dangerous slope, creaking, groaning, jolting; in one of the wagons Big Foot lay feverishly ill, coughing up blood. It took several hours to negotiate the descent. The distance wasn't all that great, maybe a few hundred feet, but they were encumbered with wagons, skittish horses, women and children, old people cramped by the cold. The logistics were impressive. Down on the flats, within easy crossing distance of the White River, the pace of the band quickened appreciably.

The morning of the twenty-fifth, a hundred years later, the sky was streaked with wafer-thin clouds, the air was ferociously cold. The walk across the tableland from the church to the rim of the pass in the company of Dana Garber, a woman from upstate New York, took about an hour. It was an easy hike across fields powdered with flaky snow and sprigged with tufts of dead grass. Dana and I positioned ourselves at an overlook on the east side of the pass where we were joined by Bob Keyes, the *Argus-Leader* reporter, who arrived by car along the park road that threads the face of the wall. Below our vantage point the road wound down the wall to the foot of the pass; directly at the spot where Big Foot's people had emerged from their descent, TV and film crews were setting up their tripods and cameras to record the reenactment of the event by the riders. Several European crews, in defiance of the prohibition issued by the *Sitanka Wokiksuye* press officers, had left the road and wandered a few yards up the pass to catch the riders as they came off the clay ridges.

The view from the overlook was impressive. Behind us, silhouetted by the rays of the morning sun, rose the crenelated outline of a weathered formation. To the south a spacious valley pimpled with flat-topped tables and buttes swept to the frozen width of the White River. To the west the asphalted ribbon of the park road curled up to the tableland, where it forked off toward the town of Wall. Located along a diagonal axis in the watershed between the White and Cheyenne Rivers, nestled in the snake-like length of a rain shadow cast by the Black Hills, the curious region known as *Mako Sica, Mauvais Terres,* the Badlands, in winter or summer, radiates a special allure. A narrow strip of cracked and peeled terrain, roughly a hundred miles long by only a few miles wide, the region over the eons has been scoured and troughed by winds and drenching rains into a maze of memorable shapes.

In the old days before the ranchers arrived, there were more springs and water holes, and therefore more grass in the Badlands. Herds of buffalo roved in and out; there were antelope, mule deer, the Audubon big horn sheep (extinct since the 1920s), gray wolves, and coyotes. No one really lived there; the leprous character of the land put most people off—"a vision of Hell after the fires have burned out," growled George Armstrong Custer. The scalded surface, twisted pinnacles, gaping pock holes, and banded ridges lent the place an eerie mystique. Indians hunted between the scaly hillocks and conducted vision quests on top of grass-crowned buttes. Ghost dancers found it a congenial place to hide. Outlaws and bandits disappeared into its depths. Long before the wars between the natives and the newcomers had ended, scientists from universities back east crept over the bald ridges and along the rubbly washes in two-wheeled carts looking for the bones of Oligocene creatures that had roamed the earth millions of years before.

By nine A.M. the riders had assembled at the edge of the Badlands Wall. They formed a line shoulder to shoulder across the snowy flats. The leaders waited on their horses a few yards in front of the riders. The point man, Ron McNeill, clearly visible in his red Pendleton coat, steered his coal-black mount to the lip of the pass. The three of us watching from the overlook held our breath. Big Foot Pass was a special place on the itinerary. It marked a rite of passage from white-owned ranchlands, edged and sectioned by barbwire and straight roads, to the convolutions of tribal ground. Tonight, riders and walkers would sleep for the first time on Indian soil, inside the reservation.

McNeill rapped his heels against the horse. Down a long, exposed, snow-streaked ridge the animal proceeded at a cautious

pace. A moment later McNeill disappeared behind an interven-
ing ridge. The leaders followed single file; behind them, funnel-
ing toward the head of the descending path like liquid toward a
spout, came the mass of more than one hundred riders. Jostling
and swaying in their saddles, they poured off the rim and down
through the complex of fissured ridges.

A few minutes later the first riders emerged near the foot of
the pass. They were close to the road, bearing down on the photographers, their horses at a run, eager to stretch their legs after
the slippery footing of the narrow trail. Exultant hoots chimed
through the air. On the overlook we shouted and waved. The
people who had parked their cars along the road cheered and
gesticulated. Singly and in bunches, hunched over like jockeys,
their arms and elbows flapping like wings, the riders galloped
across the road between the vehicles onto the table-dotted river
plain. It took a half hour for all the riders to work their way down
the pass. The last to emerge were Percy White Plume and Ron
McNeill. McNeill was the surprise. Later he admitted that he
had wanted to be first through the pass. As point man for the
riders, that was his privilege. Partway down, the trail took an
unexpected turn, which was difficult to detect. McNeill pulled
up, blocking the old path with his horse, indicating with his
finger the new route the riders should take. Whatever personal
desires he harbored were subordinate to the welfare of others.
Akicita, warrior—at Stronghold Table the previous summer,
McNeill and the other *Sitanka Wokiksuye* leaders had taken a
vow. It was their responsibility to make sure that the true meaning of the memorial ride was faithfully observed. Not only were
they to help ease the grief of what had happened at Wounded
Knee, they were to bring everyone, *wasicu* and native, into a
common bond. McNeill's job, the job of each of the leaders, was
to get behind the people and push them in the proper direction,
to lead by inspiration, to motivate by the exercise of selfless
behavior.

Nineteen eighty-six, the first year of the ride, the pass had
proven to be a formidable obstacle. The nineteen original riders
had huddled together at the edge of the lip pondering various
alternatives. "We were cold and we were scared and we couldn't

find the trail," Alex White Plume relates. "As we were looking, a pair of coyotes trotted up the spine of a narrow ridge and stopped and looked at us. Overhead, two golden eagles were circling. The coyotes looked at us awhile, then turned and trotted back down the ridge. They showed us the way. So did the eagles. Led by scouts Joe Sierra and my son Johnny Joe White Plume, we followed the path and arrived safely at the bottom of the Pass."

With the riders safely down and on their way, we turned our attention to the walkers, who, unheralded and practically unnoticed, toiled past the caravan of parked cars and up the steep slope toward the overlook. Slowly, over the yips of the last riders, came the banging of prayer drums and the indefatigable droning of the Japanese. There were maybe two dozen walkers, a mixed bunch—Indians, Asians, *wasicu*—swaddled in bulky clothing, shod in clumsy boots, marching at a steady clip. June-San and Dennis Banks led the column. Banks wore a fur cap and sheepskin coat. June-San was garbed in a gray overcoat and quilted boots; her hairless skull was covered with a green cap. She clutched the handle of a drum and tapped the taut membrane with a stick. I recognized George White Thunder by his blue jacket and the eagle feather dipping from the crown of his wool cap. The lower half of his face was wreathed in a scarf. All the walkers, with the exception of June-San and the Japanese, looked blown-out and fatigued; the savage cold had turned everyone's eyes into little pools of glue. "Come on," said Dana Garber. She tugged at my sleeve, eager to join the procession. I hesitated, though not for long. With the walkers was where I needed to be, on foot, connected to the ground, in synch with the rhythm of the trip. Bob Keyes ran an errand into Wall to call the office of the *Argus-Leader* in Sioux Falls, and I went with him, primarily to load my pockets with bags of peanuts and chocolate bars. It was Christmas morning, and the only place open was a convenience store next to Interstate 90. By noon we caught up with the walkers in the town of Interior, a half block from the faded, whitewashed building where we had spent the night. I bade Bob farewell and fell into a stiff-legged cadence between Dana and a faster from Poughkeepsie named Sherry Mattola. Famished, weak, her oval face as pale as a sheet of typing paper, Sherry struggled to maintain the pace. When she wasn't looking, I unwrapped a Heath bar and wolfed down the contents.

The sight of Interior in the brittle light brought back memories of the summer I worked at Badlands National Park. The emptiness of the town, the boom-and-bust complexion of the flimsy houses and streets, the spidery branches of the leafless trees gave off a melancholy vibration. In the early years of the century, Interior had bustled. A railroad carried people out to Rapid City and the Black Hills. A major rodeo was hosted every summer that attracted cowboys from as far away as Arizona. Then the railroad went bankrupt and the rodeo died out. The establishment of Badlands National Monument in 1939 restored a measure of economic solvency to the little town. Proximity to the reservation helped also; the *wasicu* merchants had things to sell to the Indians, namely, liquor, food, and gasoline in descending order of importance. In the early 1980s Interior boasted two taverns and a package store. In one of the taverns I took turns shooting eight ball with young Lakota guys who drifted over from the reservation. Usually I lost, but the companionship was pleasant; that, and the abiding quiet. Lakota, at least the ones I knew, play pool with little fanfare or kibitzing. The silence under the pall of blue smoke that circled the hanging lamp like a lenticular cloud was oceanic in its serenity. The embered tips of countless cigarettes danced through the murky air like fireflies. Closing time was sweetest of all. We placed the cues on the racks and muttered our goodbyes. Outside in the empty street, the wind lapping through the trees carried the doughy scent of Badlands clay, still warm from the blazing heat of the day. The silken August sky was antic with the trajectories of fiery meteors. Far out on the White River plain, coyotes howled with operatic vigor.

The walkers were strung out in a ragged line leading through town. Two vehicles chugged alongside: a van belonging to the Japanese, and a vintage four-door sedan driven by a friend of Dennis Banks. When the walkers grew numb or their legs gave out, they could sit in one of the vehicles till their strength returned and the warmth came back to their bodies.

I recognized other faces in the procession. Pagan was a New

Yorker, a young man, a faster, introverted and withdrawn. The Japanese, of course, there were ten of them, led by the indomitable June-San. Her rimless glasses seemed to magnify the iron resolve of her will. It was as if she had renounced the comeliness of her well-bred features—straight nose, flawless complexion, enticing lips—for the more important matters of world harmony and peace. Her movements were economical and precise, no superfluities or excess fluff. The woman was matchless in her dedication and zeal.

There was also, most happily, Derek Adams, an Englishman in his mid-fifties. Diminutive, compact, with a pointed goatee and lustrous blue eyes, Derek had experienced sacralized travel many times in Europe and the Himalayas. His enthusiasm was contagious, his generosity overwhelming. He had many friends on Pine Ridge; in the chore department he did a bit of everything—gofer, mechanic, dishwasher, cook, electrician.

Highway 44 out of Interior shoots straight east up a long rise before curving south to a bridge that spans the White River. It's a desolate road that seems to hang like a rope in midair. To our left, across a mile or two of snow-covered flats, loomed the ramparts of the Badlands Wall, drab and dun-colored in the feeble afternoon light. As we trudged along, the wind clawed at our clothing. At the crest of the rise an hour later we took a break. I shared a cigarette with Sherry Mattola, sucking hot smoke into my lungs. Under the layers of clothing, my limbs were coated with sweat, but the down-filled garments, high-tech underwear, and knee-length arctic parka kept the sweat from turning into ice.

Dennis Banks stood nearby, smoking. Dennis was in his mid-fifties, an Ojibway from Wisconsin. In 1972 Russell Means had invited him to Pine Ridge to help formulate a strategy to counter the terror and intimidation that had plunged the reservation into chaos. Banks was already well known in radical Indian circles; four years earlier, with another Ojibway named George Mitchell, he had founded the American Indian Movement (AIM) in Minneapolis, specifically to offer assistance to that city's neglected native population. Throughout the 1970s, by the press and in the popular imagination, Banks and Means were paired together, oft-quoted and loudly confrontational, though it was Means rather than Banks who provided the lion's share of fiery rhetoric. The two helped engineer the occupation of Wounded Knee in February of 1973 in response to the brutal murder of Raymond Yellow Thunder by white toughs in Gordon, Nebraska, and the subsequent internecine warfare that racked Pine Ridge, pitting traditionalists against mixed bloods. When the siege ended in May, Banks and Means were arrested by federal authorities. At their trial in St. Paul in 1974, the judge dismissed every charge that had been levelled against them, citing the low and underhanded tactics employed by the FBI in their apprehension. Federal and state authorities continued to harass them; they were hauled into court after court. Russell Means was eventually exonerated of thirty-nine of the forty charges brought against him. Threatened with incarceration in a South Dakota prison, where he had reason to believe that the attorney general of the state might connive to have him murdered, Banks fled to California where Governor Jerry Brown refused to extradite him to South Dakota.

By December 1990 the bitter days of the Wounded Knee siege were long gone, and, though Banks and Means could still command a modicum of attention on the reservation and in the national press, their capacity to make policy and influence lives had been drastically curtailed. There were Indians who loathed them for their involvement in the violence that engulfed Pine Ridge in the 1970s, though this was truer of Means than it was of Banks; the former, out of an instinct for grandstanding that he could not seem to curb, still went for the headlines (and would go for them again at the end of the Big Foot Ride). Standing in the middle of Highway 44 that wintry Christmas afternoon, sharing a second cigarette with Sherry, I could see why people had been drawn to Dennis Banks and would continue to be. He stood around six feet tall. His face was ruddy, his features strongly molded; a black beard flecked with gray banded a squared-off jaw. His long hair under the sheepskin cap was knotted in a queue at the base of his skull. He radiated an air of authority and resolve. There was a certifiable dignity about him, authentic and hard-won; the man wore the legend of his accomplishments like a set of ruggedly tailored clothes.

With the break over, the last cigarette squashed out, parkas once again were zipped up, gloves were pulled on, scarves and mufflers were adjusted, and in a long drawn-out file the walkers stepped along the asphalt road, this time down an incline toward the White River. I fell in next to George White Thunder, whose mood was playful. The approaching bridge jogged his memory. One time when he was around ten, he and two buddies were walking across the same bridge after sundown on a midsummer evening. Insect sounds from the trees filled the warm air with a gnashing chatter. A car or two passed, though the highway was oddly empty. A lone rider, a white fellow it looked to be, loped toward them across the bridge on a down-and-out nag. "Ugliest horse I ever saw," George said. "Maybe the oldest, too. The cowboy wore a hat pulled down over his face. It was almost dark, and we were little shavers, and we knew we had no business being out that late. We were hurrying to get to the top of the hill on the other side of the river. I had an uncle that lived there. Well, when the cowboy got almost even with us, we could see he had a cigarette stuck in his lips. Just then he touched a match to the tip, and I almost passed out. The cowboy had no eyes. Where his eyes should've been, there was two black holes. He looked over at us, just like he could see as good as anybody, and grinned and waved. You never saw three little kids hustle so fast in your life. That's a long road to the top of the hill on the other side of the bridge—you'll see for yourself in a little while. But we got there quick. I had a bad leg back then, but I beat my buddies to my uncle's house. I passed them like they was standing still."

George's giggle was contagious. I found myself smiling, forgetting the cold, imagining the cowboy, how scary his eyeless face must have looked to the three boys. "When I lived at the park, George, I heard stories about a big foot creature in these parts," I said. "The tribal police had one trapped in their headlights over in Kyle one time, but they let him get away 'cause the expression in his eyes was so human. D' you know anything about that?"

A faint grin crinkled George's lips. "Maybe," he muttered.

"I heard stories about giant tortoises that come out in the Badlands on moonlit nights and crawl around the tables and gullies. You ever hear anything about them?"

"Oh, yeah, sure." George lit a cigarette. His voice was soft, and I had to strain to catch it over the sound of the chanting and prayer drums.

"You have? Really?"

"Sure. I can take you to places. You can't see the tortoises now. It's too cold. They're asleep now. Though I bet they heard the riders today when they came down the pass."

"Where, George? Where are the places?"

It was as easy as noodling catfish in a shallow pond. George had me hooked, and he barely had to crook a finger. "Come back next summer," he said through another giggle that made his chin quiver. "I'll take you where you can see them. Don't bring a camera. They don't show up on film."

We reached the bridge and started across. The branches of the bare trees shivered in the wind. Somewhere under the bluish crust capping the river a stream of water trickled. Years ago, on a hot August afternoon, with my wife and two children, I tramped upstream from this very bridge along the several channels threading the river bed, oblivious to the heat, oblivious to the flies, oblivious to the threat of quicksand, enchanted by the chalk-white bluffs rising on the reservation side, the bank swallows darting through the air, the iridescent dragonflies looping over the sluggish current. It was like wading along a liquid, milky-gray ribbon. Our feet squished against the sandy bottom. Yelps of delight from the children echoed off the bluffs. The lactic water foaming around our ankles was as warm as blood. Cupping a handful to my nose, I found the odor musty and old, the odor of sun-baked bones. Under the weight of relentless erosion, wind and rain peeling off layer after layer of friable soil, it was as if the skeletons of countless fossils had emulsified into a sticky solution that lapped and purled through the arid heart of the Badlands. My wife threw her straw hat into the air. When a dragonfly alighted on my son's bare shoulder, he let out a shriek that sent a burly raven flapping off the top of a bluff on a ragged patter of wing strokes.

On the other side of the bridge, officially within Indian territory, Dennis Banks gathered us into a circle. He cautioned us to stay together on the road and not to lag behind. He encouraged us, when we were cold or tired, to seek relief in one of the support vehicles. The Japanese nodded understandingly. The serious expression on their faces never seemed to change. Their dedication was admirable. Despite having been at it for over six hours, they looked fresh and unruffled. Their equipment and clothing were expensive, the latest cold-weather gear. They wore designer boots and coats, fur-lined hoods, elegant gloves, and chic wool scarves. Canteens of hot tea dangled from loops attached to the straps of their day packs. They could have dropped in from a nearby ski resort. The rest of us, Indian and *wasicu*, were dressed like bumpkins. A Dakota from the Flandreau Reservation wore a Minnesota Twins ball cap bound in a goitrous knot under his chin with a ratty scarf. The man drove a produce truck through the upper Midwest. He was spending part of his vacation participating in the Wounded Knee activities. His wife was plump and shy. A fringed blanket decorated with little Easter bunnies enveloped her shoulders and back. A Minnesota Vikings stocking cap with a blue bobble fell over her left ear. Pagan, the faster from upstate New York, wore an army surplus winter coat over an eclectic layering of shirts and sweaters. The hair under the rim of his fatigue cap pronged out starchily in all directions. Sherry Mattola's ankle-length wrap was woven from strands of multicolored wool. My own outer garment was an orange deer-hunting parka so outlandishly florescent a satellite could detect it from outer space.

Dennis reminded us that tomorrow was a rest day. There would be no walking or riding. Wherever we were we could take it easy, knock back, sleep, scrounge for food. Tomorrow the fasters were scheduled to break their vigil; before sitting down finally to eat in their private tent, they would undergo a sweat bath. Tomorrow Dennis would obtain a lance with an eagle feather. It was behind this standard that we would march the rest of the way into Wounded Knee. Dennis planned to have the lance and feather blessed by Pete Catches, a renowned Oglala spiritual leader. "It will be our banner," he said. "We'll take turns carrying it. It will give us strength in the long hours ahead."

He passed around a sack of *wasna*, dried meat flavored with chokecherries, which those of us who weren't fasting devoured greedily. The stringy clot melted in my mouth like cotton candy. Almost instantly I felt invigorated. Clutching a Folger's can full of smoking sage, Dennis's young son stepped clockwise around the inside of the circle. One by one we dipped our hands into the smoke and rubbed the evanescent plumes on our arms and faces. The smoldering sage was deliciously fragrant. Renewed, we traipsed back out to the road and commenced the long climb up the slope away from the White River.

The climb was difficult. The road curved through a series of turns seeking the path of least resistance up the face of the clay-molded bluffs. At times when the incline was steep, all talking between the walkers ceased, but not the steady chanting, the steady tamping of the drum. An hour later, approaching high ground, we were rewarded with a wonderful view of the river, the ghostly ramparts of the Badlands Wall, a cluster of dwellings off to the northwest marking the town of Interior. The wind had dwindled to a whisper. The sun glittered like a spangled ornament in the western sky. In another hour it would be dark. Clumps of dry grass coiling through the snow were touched with a tawny blush. The paradox was appealing: how delicate the landscape appeared in the clutch of such a terrible cold. An eerie stillness radiated over the wrinkled crown of the bluff. A palette of tender pastels smeared the western horizon: soft yellows, faint oranges, rosy pinks.

The chanting of the Japanese helped alleviate the weight of my weary feet. Everyone was bushed; the original party had been on the go for more than eight hours. The chant, delivered over and over in the sonorous baritone of Shonosuke Ohkura, cast a welcome spell upon our labors. Each tap of the drum resounded against the tympanum of my inner ear, propelling me up the incline, step by arduous step. I tried to relax both body and mind into the lulling rhythm of drumbeat and voice. I tried not to think of anything—food, sleep, sex, tropical islands—I tried to make contact with an untapped reserve of energy that lurked beyond the discomfort of aching bunions and frozen toes. Sherry Mattola, without food now for three days, drifted along in a daze. Her eyes were partially lidded; periodically she veered off into the snow. With dogged persistence she mouthed the words of the incantation in ragged synch with Shonosuke Ohkura. I offered her my arm, but she shook it off. Her face was framed by the circle of a hood that fit snugly around her skull. Her lips were cracked and dry; the skin around her mouth puckered inward to a pair of hollow cavities that accentuated her prominent cheekbones. "Tomorrow I get to eat," she muttered.

The Little Wound School was open to riders and walkers, and after the sun went down and with only the faintest smear of light lingering in the sky, we were transported by van and Dennis's car to the town of Kyle. The fasters, including the Japanese, went on to Red Water Creek, ten miles north of Kyle, where the horses were corralled for the night and the fasters were to remain quarantined until tomorrow. Dana Garber and I toted our gear through the doors of the impressive new school and found a place at the foot of the folded-up bleachers on one side of the gymnasium. Several of the Manderson boys, including Bernard and Antoine, were sliding across the polished floor in stockinged feet, shooting baskets. The thump of the rubber ball was jarring and discordant after the placid silence of the White River valley. The gym was nowhere as crowded as the gym at the Interior school had been the night before. Kyle is located in the heart of the reservation, and many of the Big Foot Memorial participants would spend the next few nights at their homes in Porcupine, Pine Ridge, and Wanblee.

"Beezy! Hey, Beezy!" the boys called. "Come shoot baskets!"

My feet in their stiff leather boots felt as if they had been dipped in concrete. I launched the ball toward the nearest hoop and shrugged when it didn't even brush the net. Dana raised her blond eyebrows. "Some things are best left to the young," she said consolingly. I pulled my bedroll and air mattress out of my bag and inflated the mattress and stretched out with a groan at the foot of the bleachers. I thought about removing my boots, but was fearful about what might come curling off the toes of my damp socks.

"I wonder if we'll get anything to eat tonight," Dana said.

"Buffalo soup," I replied.

"Ah, yes . . ."

She stared up at the bank of lights beaming onto the court where Bernard, Antoine, and the others leaped and dribbled. I must have fallen asleep. The next thing I heard was a gentle voice. "Well, there he is. He said he was coming, and I guess he wasn't kidding."

I opened my eyes. Standing over me were Phoebe and Dominic Running Hawk. I crawled to my feet as fast as my aching joints would permit. We shook hands and embraced. Phoebe and Dominic were friends from my days at Badlands National Park. Dominic, a burly, broad-shouldered man, worked for the maintenance crew at the park. Phoebe—gentle, round-faced, soft-spoken—worked at tribal headquarters in Pine Ridge. I had written to them that I hoped to participate in the memorial ride. How they knew where to find me on Christmas night was a bit of a puzzle, but word has a way of getting around the reservation without anyone asking any questions. "We got some turkey at the house," Dominic said. "You hungry?"

Dominic and Phoebe lived in the hamlet of Porcupine, twenty miles southwest of Kyle. We drove in Dominic's Mitsubishi pickup, the three of us wedged into the cab. With all our winter clothing, the fit across the bench seat was tight. Inside the cab the air was toasty; snowflakes spattered against the windshield. We reminisced about old times, caught up on the lives of our children. The warmth from the heater made me pleasantly drowsy. The dark beyond the headlights' probe was like the dark at the bottom of a mine. We were in the moonless phase of the month, and night had settled over the reservation with an impenetrable swoop. At Sharps Corner, where we turned south, a single bulb glowed feebly from a spindly pole. A short time later, on the outskirts of Porcupine, we pulled up to a mobile home.

Phoebe heated up the remains of a turkey that family and

friends had pitched into earlier in the day. She served mashed potatoes, applesauce, rolls, and hot coffee. I ate slowly, appreciatively, trying not to smack my lips, trying not to think of Dana or Sherry or George White Thunder. Phoebe and Dominic were Catholics. Both had grown up on Pine Ridge; Phoebe's great-grandfather had died at Wounded Knee. "They're letting us off work Friday so we can watch the walkers and riders come in," she said. "I don't want to miss that."

A TV at the other end of the long room crackled with news of the outside world. Across the northern tier of midwestern states the weather was hideously cold. South Dakota was in the grip of one of the worst arctic spells in decades. Inside the mobile home, the air smelled pleasantly of turkey and hot gravy. My mind went back to the summer when my family had lived next door to Dominic's in the rangers' quarters at the park: the fun times we'd had in the evenings sitting at the picnic table in the quadrangle, watching the children scramble up the clay flanks of smooth formations to shout and wave to us from the top, their bodies awash in the golden rays of the setting sun.

"It means a lot to us that you've come all this way to be in the ride," Phoebe said. She looked down shyly at the table edge. "It's a special date for us. I lost a relative at Wounded Knee. The real story has never been told. The army has kept it secret about what happened that day. They call it a battle; they gave out lots of medals; though when you shoot down unarmed women and children, it can't be anything but a massacre, can it? If the enemy can't shoot back and you can, what do you call it?"

We talked a bit about that. I told them what I had witnessed so far on the trip. I told them I could feel something building, an emotional upwelling, a genuine desire on the part of the Indians involved to come to terms with their century-long grief, to put it aside so they could carry on into the future.

"Just to get that many Indians to cooperate on a single project is a miracle," said Dominic. "You know how we like to tear each other apart."

I spoke of the rituals I had witnessed: the drummers who performed every morning, the prayers, the repetitive circling up during the day by walkers and riders to renew their vows of commitment. "I've heard people say they can already see the spirits, that we are not alone, that every day the air is becoming more charged with the presence of the ancestors."

I told them a story that Alex White Plume had told me. On the second Big Foot Memorial Ride there were thirty-six participants. To make up for lost time on the third day they rode at night. An hour or two after dark, Alex noticed a host of luminous sparks dancing around the horses' hooves. Periodically he and Rocky Afraid of Hawk positioned themselves at the head of the line and counted the riders as they plodded by, to make sure that none had fallen or that no horse had bolted across the countryside. The sparks that whirled up from the horses' hooves were as dense as fireflies. The last time they did their tally the line of riders seemed to go on and on. The silhouettes of the riders at the back of the line were ragged and frowzy, indicating they were wrapped in furs and buffalo robes and that they carried staffs and lances. Alex and Rocky both counted eighty-six riders. By the time they counted the last one, the hair on the back of Alex White Plume's neck was electric with fright. Silently he and Rocky rode back to the head of the line. When they reached their camp an hour later and did another tally, there were only the original thirty-six riders.

"There's been good feelings all over Pine Ridge the past few days," said Phoebe. She hesitated, glancing down at her fingers pressed against the table edge. "The spirits are everywhere," she continued in a somewhat different voice. "I'm Catholic, but I'm also Indian, and I can feel them. The next few days are going to be strong. People don't realize how spiritual we Lakota are. I was up at Green Grass on Cheyenne River one time when Arvol Looking Horse and his family unwrapped the sacred pipe. They only take it out under special circumstances. When you come up to the arbor where the pipe is, you can hear the feet of thousands of buffalo pounding the earth. When you look up at the sky, you see golden eagles circling. After you back away, the buffalo stop running and the eagles stop circling."

We talked awhile longer, then bundled up, and squeezed into the pickup. Phoebe insisted on accompanying Dominic and me back to the Little Wound School. As we sped past the forlorn lamp at Sharps Corner, the void of the winter night engulfed us with a subterranean depth. It was as dark as I could remember anything ever being in my life, gallows dark, sedimentary dark, as if the earth had turned itself inside out, and instead of riding across its surface, we were boring through its core. Dominic's voice, steady and gentle, filled the cab. "When I cross the river in the morning on my way to the park, I feel like I'm going into another country. The park's not that far from Porcupine. The land doesn't change that much, but there's a difference. It's no longer Indian land. It belongs to someone else. Driving home in the evening, as the road bends past Kyle toward the buttes behind Porcupine, I feel good. The heart is here. I can hear that heart beating no matter where I am. I heard it in Korea when I was stationed there. I heard it in California when I lived out there. I can hear it now, through the darkness, in the cold, with everything dead and brown and the wind as sharp as a weasel's tooth."

He paused. The silence washed between the frosty windows. Dominic's voice when he spoke again was quick and breathy. "If you cut off a turtle's head, the heart beats for days. The heart is stronger than the turtle's head. It seems funny, but that's the way it is. We got lots of turtles around here. Men and women with no heads whose hearts just keep on beating. You've met a few already. Before this thing is over, you'll be meeting a few more."

6

With the melting away of Big Foot's band into the hills south of the Cheyenne River, the situation between the military and the Indians in South Dakota took a turn for the worst. Each mile the Miniconjous drew closer to Pine Ridge increased their chances of running into serious trouble—not because of any prearranged plan on the part of the army to bring them to grief, but because of the perils inherent in a band of armed Indians on the move in frontier America. At their camp on the Cheyenne River, stationary and peaceful, within easy monitoring distance of Colonel Sumner's troop, the Miniconjous were removed from any temptation that might possibly get them into trouble. On the go, their whereabouts unknown, they posed a different problem; their vanishing act under Sumner's nose not only caused that officer to be rebuked by his superiors, but led to an uproar in the newspapers and aggravated the worst fears of the settlers.

A band of mobile Indians, armed with Winchesters, no matter how burdened by the presence of women and children, no matter how peacefully inclined, was a distinct threat to the new sedentary order of Great Plains life.

The disturbances on the South Dakota reservations in the summer and fall of 1890 provided a source of distraction for a national population that had doubled to nearly seventy million in the quarter century since the end of the Civil War. Communications had improved dramatically during that period. Telegraph wires spanned the coasts; a primitive telephone line operated between Pine Ridge and Rushville, Nebraska, though it didn't work very well and was eventually abandoned in favor of the more reliable telegraph. By early December nearly one-third of the available troops in the U.S. military had been sent to the Dakotas. The largest concentration of men and material since the end of the Civil War was big news indeed, and throughout the fall of 1890 correspondents flocked to Pine Ridge and the nearby border towns to file reports to newspapers all over the country.

Following the Civil War the newspaper business underwent a period of unprecedented expansion. Between 1870 and 1900 the number of dailies in the United States quadrupled, and their combined circulation increased six-fold, primarily because of the upsurge in urban population, a rise in overall literacy, and a rapidly expanding advertising market. During the lull that followed the initial buildup of troops in early November, reporters covering the Ghost Dance were exhorted by their editors to write stories about war-crazed savages that would whet the appetites of white readers in St. Louis and Chicago. Gilbert Bailey, correspondent for the *Rocky Mountain News*, was bombarded by demands from his editor to produce "more blood." Thomas Tibbles of the *Omaha World Herald* provoked his editor's wrath when he "absolutely refused to manufacture tales about a 'war' which simply did not exist." The editor ordered Tibbles to return to Omaha, calling him a "complete failure." The correspondents' dilemma was best summed up by Charles Seymour of the *Chicago Herald*, who in frustration penned the following bit of doggerel:

All silent lies the village,
On the bosom of the vale,
So I'll squeeze another pipe-dream,
And grind out another tale.

Editors thought nothing of livening up their correspondents' colorless dispatches with details culled from the copy of less responsible journalists, who willingly fed their editors all the hyperbole they wanted. It was the age of yellow journalism; the object was to sell as many newspapers as possible. Headlines such as "In a State of Terror/Indians Dancing With Guns" *(Chicago Daily Tribune)* and "The Messiah Expected to Arrive at the Pine Ridge Agency Today, When the Savages Will Fight" *(New York Times)* were commonplace.

L. Frank Baum, future creator of *The Wizard of Oz*, an author who, in his later years, would be lionized by the public for his sensitivity to the feelings of children, vented his spleen against the Indians in an editorial in the *Aberdeen (South Dakota) Saturday Pioneer* on December 20, 1890: "Why not annihilation? Their glory has fled, their spirit broken, their manhood effaced; better that they should die than live the miserable wretches they are . . . The whites, by law of conquest, by justice of civilization, are masters of the American continent."

Embittered over the failure of a merchandise mart he had founded in Aberdeen, Baum took his wrath out on the poor and disenfranchised of the Dakota territory, Indians as well as white farmers who had gone under as a result of drought, bank failures, and grasshopper plagues. Ironically, as a newspaper man, Baum was considered a "progressive." He espoused the new industrialism and applauded the growth of consumerism. He took up the cudgels on behalf of such radical issues as women's suffrage. In an editorial in the *Saturday Pioneer* on February 1, 1890, he wrote, "The key to success of our country is tolerance." Evidently that "tolerance" did not extend to Indians or to the ordinary *wasicu* sodbuster.

The fulsome rhetoric dished up by columnists and editors was contagious. An official who should have known better, General Nelson A. Miles, issued a spurious announcement of his own on December 2: "The seriousness of the situation at [Pine Ridge] has not been exaggerated. The disaffection is more widespread than it has been at any time for years. The conspiracy extends to more different tribes than have heretofore been hostile, but they are now in full sympathy with each other and are scattered over a larger area of country than in the whole history of Indian warfare. It is a more comprehensive plot than anything ever inspired by the Prophet or Tecumseh or even Pontiac."

Another facet of the newspaper coverage required Miles's attention. A decade of reservation life had produced a number of literate Indians. Young men attending schools such as Carlisle in Pennsylvania could read and write English with fluent ease. Information about troop movements appearing in regional newspapers was monitored by them and then shared at tribal councils. To protect the army, secrecy was necessary; on November 17, Miles refused to divulge to the press details of a major troop movement to both the Pine Ridge and Rosebud Reservations. Hostilities between natives and whites were no longer the simple clash of alien cultures they had been during Sitting Bull's war of 1876–77; a decade of reservation life had produced a cadre of Indians who could think and talk like white people.

As the troops poured in, the towns bordering the reservations experienced a boom which helped pull their economies out of the doldrums in which they had languished for most of the 1880s. So miffed were the merchants of Chadron, Nebraska, at the commercial success of the rival towns of Gordon and Rushville that they sent a delegation all the way to Washington to petition Major General John M. Schofield, commander in chief of the U.S. Army, to throw a little business their way.

The complexities of these money matters were lost on Big Foot and his troop, who, as of December 23, had struck out on their own across the landscape. At his headquarters in Rapid City, General Miles was furious with Colonel Sumner for letting the Miniconjous slip from his grasp. With Big Foot rolling around South Dakota like a loose cannon, the general's carefully crafted plans to contain a major outbreak were thrown in jeopardy. Friendly Pine Ridge chiefs had agreed to send five hundred warriors in a show of strength to Stronghold Table to persuade

Ghost Dance stalwarts Short Bull and Kicking Bear to give up the craze and come in; Miles was fearful that Big Foot, in his words "very cunning and very bad," would link up with the stalwarts and ruin any chances for a peaceful solution to the problem. Junior officers gave the general a wide berth as he paced, fuming and muttering, around the terrazzo floor of the lobby of the Harney Hotel. Miles's blood was up; he vowed to bring in the renegade Indians if it was the last thing he did.

For Miles, personally and professionally, there was a lot at stake. His reputation as an Indian fighter was considerable: in the wake of the disaster at Little Big Horn, he had been instrumental in bringing hostile Lakota and Cheyenne factions to bay; he had also tracked down Chief Joseph, the legendary Nez Perce leader, when he tried to lead his people to the safety of Canada in 1877. But for all his vaunted successes, Miles was afflicted with a crippling pride and outspoken vanity that galled his superiors and irritated his peers in the officer corps.

Miles came from undistinguished Boston origins; he worked as a clerk in a crockery store before the Civil War. He was ambitious, and the war helped fuel his desire for recognition and power. By the time Appomattox rolled around, he had achieved the brevet rank of brigadier general of volunteers; at Fort Monroe, Virginia, eager to gain the good wishes of his superiors, he had taken on the onerous duty of personally supervising the incarceration of Jefferson Davis, ex-president of the Confederate States of America. Vengeful Republicans, in the aftermath of Lincoln's assassination, wanted to make certain the former leader was properly chastised for his role in the rebellion, and Miles— anxious to obtain a commission in the postwar regular army— translated that wish into a reality that at times bordered upon the sadistic. Certain actions guaranteed to humiliate the proud and sensitive Davis, such as having his ankles shackled in irons, were left to Miles's discretion. "A beast," Varina Davis, wife of the Confederate chief, wrote later in an outburst of righteous indignation. "A hyena, and only 26 years old."

That first night, December 23, 1890, Big Foot's band traveled hard and fast. The air was piercingly cold. The night was so gloomy that a lantern man had to walk ahead of the procession to lead the way; other lanterns were posted along the line of vehicles and horses so the rest of the party could follow. Snow flurries made things more difficult. In spite of these obstacles the Indians moved so rapidly that before daylight they had covered nearly thirty miles. They found a sheltered place on the north fork of the Bad River (near Fred McDaniels' ranch today), where they halted for a few hours.

Shortly after daybreak, under clearing skies, with the wind whipping at a vicious clip, they started off again. The pace they set was relentless. By midafternoon the band reached the edge of the Badlands Wall. With men working fast out front, smoothing the crumbly slope with picks and shovels, the wagons were guided safely down the pass. Before dark the party crossed the White River and made camp on the other side. Though still some fifty miles from Pine Ridge, they were on reservation soil. Their diligence paid off; all day Colonel E. A. Carr's Sixth Cavalry had hunted the Miniconjous north of the Badlands Wall. Unable to believe the Indians could have come so far in so short a time, Carr's men continued their search to the north the following day.

That night, Christmas Eve, in camp on the White River, Big Foot's sickness settled into pneumonia. The next morning he was so ill the Miniconjous moved only eight miles to a place called Cedar Spring (today known as Big Foot Springs). From there three riders were sent out to Pine Ridge with the news that the Miniconjou chief had reached the reservation and, despite the fact that he was desperately ill, was on his way to join Red Cloud and the other Oglala leaders.

All night a powerful wind scoured the bare hills. The morning sky was streaked with scudding clouds. The wind was so strong it jerked tents and tipis out of the ground and sent them tumbling. Through blasts of alkali dust the Indians toiled. After four troublesome miles they finally halted in the shelter of a bluff at Medicine Root Creek (near where the town of Kyle now stands). Next morning the wind eased; with the mercurial quickness that is the hallmark of weather change on the Northern Plains, the air was mild and tolerable. Before the Miniconjous broke camp, the three riders returned from Pine Ridge. The chiefs there warned Big Foot that a detachment of Seventh Cavalry bivouacked along Wounded Knee Creek was waiting to intercept him. The chiefs advised that he swing east and south to avoid detection; Big Foot, his lungs rheumy, his breath coming in labored gasps, overruled his headmen and ordered the party to steer directly for Pine Ridge. On into the night, guided by the light of a soap-white moon, they plodded. While it was still dark a halt was finally called at the deserted settlement of American Horse. The Miniconjous were a day's march from Pine Ridge.

There was money in it for whomever spotted them first, fifty dollars, two months extra pay, half donated by the army, half by the pool of correspondents in Pine Ridge, who were eager to make something happen. December 28, a Sunday, was unseasonably mild. While stopped for lunch along Porcupine Creek, the Miniconjous were sighted by four Oglala scouts in the employ of the U.S. Army. (Whether the four ever shared the reward remains unknown.) Two of the scouts hustled back to the Seventh Cavalry bivouac along Wounded Knee Creek, four miles to the south. Major Samuel Whitside sounded boots and saddles, and four troops of bluecoats swung onto their horses. Early in the afternoon the two sides made contact on the slope of a hill south of Porcupine Creek, a spot which today is commemorated by a historical marker. Major Whitside did not like what he saw. Big Foot's warriors were clearly belligerent; they had tied up the tails of their ponies and were galloping them back and forth in front of the wagons to obtain their second wind, as was customary before a battle. Whitside ordered his men to fan out in a skirmish line; the two Hotchkiss guns (rapid-fire cannon) were unlimbered and wheeled into position to provide covering fire.

It appeared as if violence might erupt. Then a wagon bearing a white flag bumped and creaked through the line of racing warriors and banged and jolted over the hard, uneven ground. Inside the wagon lay Big Foot. Major Whitside rode out in front of his own scouts. Without dismounting, he leaned into the wagon and shook the sick man's hand. Though he had been told the chief had come to Pine Ridge on a warlike mission, seeing him in the back of the wagon, bundled up in a blood-stained blanket, made the major question the caliber of his own information. Big Foot raised up when the officer took his hand. Spots of blood had congealed on the plank floor. "I come on a mission of peace," Big Foot said in a croaky voice. "The Pine Ridge chiefs are quarreling between themselves. They are quarreling with the white chiefs. I have come to try and bring peace between all of them."

Though under strict orders to disarm the warriors, Major Whitside was fortunately dissuaded from doing so by the strenuous objections of his chief scout, a mixed blood named John Shangreau, who protested that such a move would only lead to bloodshed. Whitside, recognizing the sensibleness of Shangreau's argument, wisely demurred. (Would that Colonel Forsyth the following morning had followed the same advice!) Disarmament could come at a later time, in a more secure situation, with fewer women and children present, under the authority of an officer whose rank was superior to Whitside's. The major had the sick chief transferred to a more comfortable wagon. The troopers cradling the chief's frail form in its sling of dirty blankets tried to place him inside the military ambulance as gently as possible. By the time the transfer was completed the sun was low on the western horizon. Flanked by bluecoats maintaining a wary distance, the train of weary Miniconjous clattered over the hills and down into the spacious, bowl-shaped valley threaded by Wounded Knee Creek.

The sight of the starched white rows of Sibley tents neatly arrayed at the foot of a knoll must have preyed uneasily on the Indians' minds. They were herded onto a level stretch of ground between the knoll and a wide ravine, where they were told to set up their tents and tipis. Chief Big Foot, wretchedly sick by this time, was carted into a walled tent with a wood-burning stove. Ponies and horses were driven into a makeshift corral to the west of the encampment; inexplicably, only young boys were allowed to bring water from the creek. Cook fires flared up; rations were issued, blankets, distributed. When the adults tried to fill their pails and buckets, they were turned away by sentries patrolling the perimeter of the camp. The tightness of the security intensified the Indians' fears. Night closed down swiftly. Mules toiled up the brow of the knoll northwest of the camp, dragging a pair of Hotchkiss guns and boxes of ammunition.

In the wretched darkness of the winter evening four more troops of Seventh Cavalry arrived from Pine Ridge and went into camp next to the Miniconjous. Two more Hotchkiss guns and additional boxes of ammunition were hauled to the top of the knoll. Horses whinnied and stamped; orders rang out; cook fires crackled; bayonets clicked into place as new sentries came on duty. In the Miniconjou camp, despite their fatigue, there was a feeling of uncertainty. The troop buildup, the quartet of cannon peering down from the knoll, the multiple guards posted along the perimeter did not bode well for tomorrow. In addition, the mood in the bluecoat camp was disturbingly festive. Elated messages had already been sent to General Miles in Rapid City. The capture of Big Foot was being viewed by some as the final chapter in the long history of the Indian wars. A whiskey wagon had come out from Pine Ridge, and some of the officers were getting ready to toast the occasion in proper fashion. Colonel James W. Forsyth, commander of the Seventh Cavalry, was on hand to assume personal responsibility for the disarmament of the Indians the following morning.

The Seventh Cavalry, Custer's old outfit, was one of the most storied units in the U.S. Army. Fourteen and a half years had elapsed since that fateful day along the Little Big Horn when 269 men had been wiped out in an onslaught of Plains Indian warriors. Present that night in the encampment of bluecoats along Wounded Knee Creek were a handful of officers and NCOs who had survived the battle: men who had made a career out of warring with Native Americans in dozens of battles and skirmishes, men who had seen their comrades mutilated and scalped and who had perpetrated atrocities of their own. Present also, subtly but unmistakably, was the taint of a lingering grudge against warriors like Big Foot who had fought at Little Big Horn.

The function of the U.S. Army had changed significantly since 1865. Mass demobilization in the wake of Appomattox left a handful of regiments with which to police the defeated South and to pacify the Indians west of the Mississippi River. From

1865 to 1877 the army's primary role in the West was to subdue bands of disgruntled natives and herd them onto reservations where missionaries and schoolteachers could acculturate them to the ways of *wasicu* life. Staffed with a mix of Civil War veterans, old-time regulars, and immigrant recruits, the army was an organization which, in nearly every skirmish or battle during those years, confronted an enemy of equal size, experience, and leadership skills.

By 1890 the makeup of this fighting force had changed; the enemy it faced had also changed. Indian tribes no longer wandered at will over the landscape; the majority of their best leaders had been killed or imprisoned. The reservations they had been forced onto were hedged in by white settlements, reinforced by a protective ring of forts, linked together by telegraph. By 1890 an interlocking grid of squares and rectangles had been superimposed upon the circular immensity of what once had been a mythical landscape. The primary component of this grid was a network of railroads which, in addition to bringing in new settlers to fill the empty spaces, also expedited the movement of military units from one trouble spot to the next. Colonel E. A. Carr's Sixth Cavalry, which had searched for Big Foot north of the Badlands Wall, had been transported from its regimental headquarters in New Mexico—eight companies, 450 men and 21 officers, plus all their horses, vehicles, and forage—in less than a week in early December; the same journey in 1876 would have taken a month or more to complete.

By 1890 the army served as a kind of mobile police force. Indians weren't the only dissidents to be dealt with in *fin-de-siècle* America; increasingly the army was called upon by federal authorities to quell outbreaks of civil strife around the country. Race riots, railroad strikes, industrial protests, and mining disputes required the services of a roving constabulary professionally trained to uphold law and order and to protect private property. In July of 1877 President Rutherford B. Hays sent federal troops to settle a strike on the Baltimore & Ohio Railroad at Martinsburg, West Virginia. Later that month, when the rail yard in Pittsburgh was blocked by protesting workers, six hundred troops opened fire, killing twenty-six people. In the wake of a bomb that exploded in Haymarket Square in Chicago in 1886, killing police and protestors and triggering a savage outburst of violence, federal troops were rushed by train to help enforce martial law.

From an instrument of frontier pacification, the army had evolved into an instrument of dissident coercion. Post–Civil War America was convulsed in turmoil generated by the final settling of the West and the unwillingness of industrial entrepreneurs to better the wages and working conditions of their (largely) immigrant laborers. In the midst of this period of turbulent expansion, gold was discovered in the Black Hills in 1874. The potential for enriching the national coffers was too tempting to ignore; an influx of precious ore could help the economy recover from the Depression of 1873 (the most devastating and prolonged in the country's history). On November 3, 1875, President Ulysses Grant, General Philip Sheridan, Secretary of War William Belknap, and Secretary of Interior Zachariah Chandler met at the White House and decided to rescind the order forbidding miners and homesteaders from entering the Black Hills. With this unilateral abrogation of the 1868 Treaty, the fate of the Lakota and their Cheyenne and Arapaho allies was sealed. The mass of territory encompassing portions of five states, with the Black Hills anchoring the center like a granite spike—which had been deeded to the Indians by a legal agreement ratified by the U.S. Senate—was thrown open to white exploitation. The so-called "peace policy" of the first seven years of the Grant administration, which had emphasized restraint and accommodation, was replaced by a relentless effort by hardliners to disenfranchise trans-Mississippi Indians of their ancestral lands.

The majority of the enlisted men of the Seventh Cavalry who camped along Wounded Knee Creek that final night had never experienced combat or been in danger from any hostile force, Indian or otherwise. Eighty of the men, or about one-fifth of the total force, were brand new inductees, immigrants either from Europe or from the slums of Eastern cities; they were in their late teens or early twenties, and they were largely ignorant of Indians. Of these, maybe half had been in the army for a month and barely knew how to ride a horse. South Dakota in late December was a desolate and lonely place. The men were frightened, and they were cold. The discipline imposed upon them by their officers was harsh.

The evening of December 28, 1890, four more troops of Seventh Cavalry arrived from Pine Ridge and took up positions around the perimeter of the Miniconjou camp. Unlike Indian ponies, cavalry horses were shod with iron shoes, and the sound the arriving columns made against the frozen earth was like the sharp tattoo of drums. Campfires flickered in the moonless night. From the trees fringing Wounded Knee Creek came the hooting of an owl. Slowly, uneasily, Big Foot's people covered their shivering limbs with blankets and lay down to sleep. In a well-lit tent heated by a wood-burning stove, several of the older officers who'd survived the assault against Major Reno's company that terrible day in 1876 along the Little Big Horn filled their tin cups with whiskey and began reminiscing about old times.

7

The weather was bitter cold. Civil War veterans said the campaign was the hardest they had ever experienced. Fording icy rivers, sleeping tentless in the snow, making forced marches through sleet and gale in sub-zero temperatures, riding in isolated troops . . .

Pershing never forgot the freezing weather. When an officer drew a pint of whiskey from his pocket, his fingers were so numb that it fell on a rock and splattered on the snow. A shivering enlisted man chattered, "Sir, have I your permission to eat that snow?"

To protect themselves against the cold, men devoured tremendous quantities of food. Breakfast was a large pie plate heaped with bacon, beans, and hard-bread washed down with a quart of steaming coffee; lunch, whatever could be stuffed into the saddle bags and eaten on the way; supper, heaps of beef, potatoes, and other substantials. "I could not now eat in four days what I did then in one," Pershing said later. He gained twenty pounds in two months.

—*Donald Smythe,* Guerrilla Warrior: The Early Life of John J. Pershing *(1973)*

The following morning, in Bob Keyes's car, we drove out to Red Water Camp, a few miles north of Kyle. The camp was pleasantly situated in a small valley ringed by sheltering hills. Scores of horses penned in a spacious corral nickered and stamped their feet. Tents and tipis dotted the level campsite nestled between the hills. Smoke plumed out of the stem of a metal pipe sticking up from the fasters' tent. The morning air was lit with tepid sunshine. The temperature was tucked well below zero, but no wind blew, at least not down in this snug hollow. Our boots in the hard-packed snow made a sound like crisp celery being crunched at a fancy party. The dry air amplified the faintest sounds: the slushy vocables of Lakota passing between two men working over a set of harnessing, the snort and stomp of the horses, the crack of logs disintegrating in a fire, the shrill whine of a buzz saw.

The fasters were scheduled to end their ordeal today. Before they sat down to feast, they had to go through an *inipi,* or sweat lodge ceremony. Several people, under Wilmer Stampede's watchful eye, were putting the finishing touches to a sweat lodge in a clearing between two stands of leafless cottonwoods. Bob and I scooped up armloads of hay from a disintegrating bale and spread them out on the rounded sides and shoved handfuls down around the base to seal off any cracks that might permit daylight to seep inside. The boughs of the mound-shaped lodge were bent practically at right angles. Around their supporting frame a heavy sheet of green canvas had been carefully wrapped. In a pit a few feet in front of the entrance a pile of rocks lay baking in the smoldering fire.

The fasters would be purified in two shifts, men first, led by Wilmer, then the women. The male fasters stood uncomfortably around the pit: George White Thunder, Pagan, a trio of Lakota riders, tough young guys, one with his shirt already removed, bare-chested in the sub-zero air. Two sun dance scars glistened like chalk marks above his dark nipples. Four Japanese stood at the edge of the pit. They were trim and well mannered, and they stared hungrily into the fire as if trying to absorb its warmth with the suction of their eyes. Directly in front of the entrance was a buffalo skull altar. Wilmer Stampede knelt beside it, clutching a long-stemmed pipe capped with a blood-red catlinite bowl. His lips fluttered soundlessly as he muttered a prayer. To the six directions in a careful motion he offered the pipe; then he packed the bowl with scraps of *kinnickkinick* (a mixture of tobacco and red willow or cedar bark). Standing up, with a sweeping motion, he offered the pipe again to the cardinal directions. Bob and I watched attentively. So did the shivering fasters. Suddenly—and I'm certain I didn't imagine this; Bob turned as quickly as I did toward the cottonwoods directly behind us—a bird called from a tree down by the creek. Midwinter, arctic temperatures, the air was as dry as a moccasin heel. I thought I saw Wilmer smile. A subtle noise like the chirring of a cicada escaped his lips. He peeled off his ankle-length great goat; other than a towel banding his waist, he was naked underneath. He nodded to the fasters, and crouching on all fours, he entered the lodge through the open flap. The fasters hastily disrobed. In a few minutes they would be baking in suffocating heat, drawing draughts of scalding air into their lungs. On all fours now, in a line, like children following one another on a dare, they disappeared into the lodge. Wilmer's muffled voice, directing them where to sit, drifted out the open flap into the windless air. The last thing Bob and I saw as we started toward the car was the custodian—an old man, hatless, with bowed arms and a barrel chest loosely bound in a gray sweater—hefting a white-hot stone flaked with pearly ashes on a pronged stick toward the sweat lodge door.

At the Little Wound School we picked up Dana Garber and Ulbo de Sitter and headed out for the town of Pine Ridge. Ulbo, known as Bo, was a photojournalist from Amsterdam, a personable young man in his mid-twenties, knowledgeable and articulate. He'd persuaded one of the bigger weekly magazines in the Netherlands to fly him to New York; from there he had financed his own way out to Rapid City. That first day Bo had accompanied the riders; by midday his camera shutter had iced over and he started jotting down things in a notebook with cramped fingers. Bo was tall and thin, with a modish European burr haircut; he had sharply chiseled features and hazel-colored eyes.

Our destination was Big Bat's in Pine Ridge. It was our day off, and we were famished (even after stuffing myself at the Running Hawk's the night before, I was still ravenous); we intended to gorge ourselves on hamburgers and french fries. "I got to scarf some junk," Bob Keyes announced with a theatrical waggle of the fingers across his parted lips. "I'm so hungry I could eat a buttered skunk."

The first leg of the forty-mile drive recapped the drive the night before to the Running Hawk's. We went west out of Kyle, down a long curving slope to the turnoff for Sharps Corner, past Oglala Lakota College, then up and down ten miles over an undulating road. A few miles from the junction with the Porcupine road, we came upon an impressive sight. The sky was streaked with trailing clouds; the sun beamed with feeble intensity from a spot way off on the southern horizon. The bluffs behind the hamlets of Evergreen and Porcupine were sheeted with frozen snow, their summits shadowed with pinion and juniper. Something about this stretch of road always captured my fancy. Cresting the top of a hill, we caught a glimpse to the north of the jagged escarpment of the Badlands. To the south spread the tangle of buttes and hills that formed the watershed between Porcupine and Wounded Knee Creeks. Rumor had it that Crazy Horse was buried in this region. Some people say the warrior was buried along Beaver Creek Valley in northwest Nebraska. The exact location is unknown. Crazy Horse died at Fort Robinson, Nebraska, during the night of September 6, 1877, after being bayoneted in a scuffle with Indian police and white soldiers who had taken him prisoner. The following afternoon his parents carted the body on a travois into the hills northeast of the fort. Friends followed at a distance, though not too close; the parents remained alone with their dead son and their terrible grief. In a valley bounded by high-crowned bluffs, the body was secured to the limbs of a burial tree. A spirit bundle containing personal items and a lock of hair was assembled by Crazy Horse's father. (After fasting on Bear Butte, after receiving a vision foretelling his son's greatness, the older man had given his son his own name.) A day and night of mourning passed; the body was taken down from the tree and transported by travois to a place, some people say, near Wounded Knee Creek. In a crevice between two bluffs, so the story goes, the mortal remains were interred in an upright position facing west. The crevice was then packed with rocks and debris, the opening thoroughly camouflaged.

Big Bat's was new to the reservation since I was there last, an amply stocked convenience store and cafe located on the main drag across from tribal headquarters. We tramped in, took a booth, and started ordering. Everything looked delicious, including the ketchup in slick plastic packets; it takes lots of energy to offset the effects of extreme cold, and over the past few days that energy had about spent itself. We needed to build it back up. We needed to regenerate our metabolic batteries with generous doses of grease and processed beef and dehydrated potatoes, which we proceeded diligently to do. Cheeseburgers, hot dogs, french fries, onion rings, supplemented by tuna sandwiches, dinner salads, scrambled eggs, sides of bacon and sausage, hash browns, toast, washed down with hot coffee, washed down with hot tea, washed down with Pepsis and Cokes—this cholesteric feast we topped off with ice-cream sundaes, Fudgesicles, and crunchy Heath bars. We ate till we couldn't stuff another morsel down our gullets. We ate till our cheeks glistened, till our bulky clothes were spattered with condiments, till the table looked like a messy landfill. We took bites of each other's food; we dunked french fries in little cups of mayonnaise; we dabbed mustard on tuna fish; we mixed ice cream with onion rings. Every scrap tasted heavenly. Every fried, baked, breaded, or broiled bit tasted as heavenly to our famished palates as that first buffalo in early spring must have to Lakota hunters after they had slain it with a bow and arrow. Trembling with anticipation, ravenous after being holed up all winter, they leaped off their ponies and slit the belly with their knives and drew forth the steaming entrails, which they pinched between their fingers before tearing off pieces with their teeth. The organs were next—liver, kidneys, heart—which they devoured raw in blood-slick chunks, and then the swollen stomach bladder, tumescent with tender young grass, which parted with a soft plupping sound under the point of the knife to reveal a mass of stems and blades decomposed into a sticky chlorophyll stew.

The streets of Pine Ridge that frosty afternoon were deserted. A few people drifted into Big Bat's to eat and drink coffee. The daily edition of the *Rapid City Journal* contained a story about the riders and walkers, how far they had come, how far they had left to go; the story reported that the weather was unbearable. In contrast to summer, when the street outside was thronged with people, there wasn't a whole lot going on in Pine Ridge this particular Wednesday afternoon. The brick buildings housing the tribal offices looked bleak and deserted. The trees lining the street were as thin and stiff as dried toothpicks. It was the Moon of Popping Trees, when limbs compressed by the icy air were known to explode with the sharp crack of a high-powered rifle.

Pine Ridge is a hard-ass town, a mix of bureaucratic arrogance and welfare belligerence. It has the feel of government towns everywhere: snotty and on the make, steeped in intrigue and deal-making, cocky with the certainty of its own power. Full bloods and traditionalists dislike the place. Descendants of the "loafers" live there—that faction of the Oglala, composed primarily of mixed bloods, who, since the time of first contact along the Oregon Trail in the 1850s, settled near the forts so they could obtain whiskey and rations. Pine Ridge was also the final home of Red Cloud, an outstanding nineteenth-century chief. A bold warrior in his youth, Red Cloud had scored a stunning victory over the U.S. Cavalry, which led to the abandonment of a string of forts along the Bozeman Trail in eastern Wyoming and the signing of the controversial Treaty of 1868. When barely in his twenties, Red Cloud killed a powerful chief named Bear Bull in a drunken brawl. The brawl drove a wedge between the Oglalas and divided them along factional lines that persist to this day. Bear Bull's son was Little Wound, after whom the school in Kyle was named. For the rest of their lives, Little Wound and his followers remained rivals with Red Cloud and his people.

Blood feuds among the Lakota are epic in their duration and intensity. Little Wound was a progressive, an Episcopalian, who worked to ease the painful transition between the old ways and the new. Red Cloud, a complex man torn by ambivalent feelings, resisted change until the 1870s, after which he began to negotiate with the white invaders. Federal emissaries, seeking to defraud both factions of their land, cleverly played off one leader against the other. Today, to many people in the outlying districts, Pine Ridge symbolizes everything bad that's ever happened to the tribe. "They're like a bunch of maggots over there," growled a full blood I know from Rocky Ford, who lives in a log house at the edge of the Badlands, "feasting on the poisoned carcass of the white man's government."

In the car on the way back to Kyle there was more talk of food. We sat with swollen bellies, staring out the windows. It was late afternoon; a delicate purple light seeped out of the draws and valleys of the snow-mantled slopes. Bob Keyes reminded us of the fact that, in the absence of proper forage, warriors in the old days had fed their ponies the bark from cottonwood trees. Bob's remark reminded me of something else. "They ate every part of the buffalo," I added. "The testicles were considered a delicacy. If they killed a pregnant female, they boiled the fetus in water from the uterus and ate every bit of the fetus and drank every drop of the water."

A sigh escaped someone's lips in the back seat. A gust of wind slammed into the side of the car, rocking it on its wheels. Lost in thought, mindful of what lay ahead tomorrow, we sped on toward the gloomy shadows that rose out of the east like a devouring mouth.

Thursday morning Dana, Bob, and I put on our warmest clothing, and in Bob's car, numb with sleep, groggy from the effects of a junk-food hangover, we motored out to Red Water Creek. It was already light when we arrived. The air was sullenly cold. Several riders lurched around the corral swinging lariats, trying to cut their horses from the pack. A minor disaster had occurred during the night; someone had left the corral gate open, and twenty to thirty horses had vanished into the frozen countryside. By 8:00 A.M. the horses still had not been located. People were out looking for them in vehicles; a private plane was winging over the district. Despite the implications, the *Sitanka Wokiksuye* leaders on hand that morning did not seem too upset. "We'll get 'em back," said Birgil Kills Straight with an indulgent grin. He might have been speaking about a bunch of truant school kids. "D' you suppose they got a little too much rest yesterday?"

Dennis Banks, June-San, and the Japanese arrived. The fasters—Pagan, Sherry, and George White Thunder, among others—stepped sleepily out of their tent. They looked rested and relaxed. After the sweat yesterday, they had sat down in the tent to a meal of buffalo stew, fresh vegetables, fry bread, and plum pudding. The expression on George's face as he described the food was positively rapturous. Though the Japanese had ended their fast, they did not seem as elated. June-San was itching to get started this morning. She squinched her face into a bossy pout and barked what sounded like a list of instructions to her companions. Dennis Banks remained unfazed by her sense of urgency. He pulled a glazed donut out of a droopy pocket hanging at the side of his sheepskin coat and munched it tranquilly. Then, licking his lips, he called for the walkers to circle up.

We offered a prayer, then broke circle, and wound away from the camp, up the gashed and rutted road toward the summit of a sheltering hill. The road snaked across a series of hills before cresting a watershed and slanting down toward the asphalt highway. June-San and her group set a vigorous pace. Up and down over the bald hills ringing the hollow of a Red Water Creek we tramped, first in a compact file, then, as the hills became steeper and the wind picked up, in a line that began to unravel. Axel Koester had injured his ankle, and despite his youth and generous stride, he fell behind, hobbled by a painful limp. Though the air was bright, the sun offered no appreciable warmth. The cold began to press against us like a knuckled fist.

It took a couple of hours to reach the asphalt road. The morning sky was streaked with filmy clouds; the sun continued to beam, albeit feebly, like a low-watt bulb. The wind commenced to probe and dig. Sweeping in from the northwest at a steady whistle, it tore at our clothing and clawed at our legs. After a brief rest to permit the stragglers to catch up, we started south along the asphalt road in the direction of Kyle. June-San continued to set a fast pace, and I began to understand why. Down off the hills, the walk took on a new seriousness. Kyle was eight miles away. Fortunately, the terrain was fairly level. Unfortunately, the country to the west opened with an expansive sweep, presenting few obstacles to the wind. By ten o'clock the air was howling. Clouds of stinging snow blasted across the road. The gusts caught our padded figures and pushed us like sails toward a steep ditch on the left. After an hour of leaning against this hard force, I was exhausted. Despite the layers of underwear and wool pants and lumberjack shirts and insulating parka, I could feel the cold creeping like a clammy gel across my limbs. Under pressure of the relentless wind, the line of walkers began to disintegrate. Dana dropped out. Axel disappeared behind a veil of snow. The chanting of the Japanese was swallowed up by the angry blasts.

By the fourth hour the walk was no longer a pilgrimage but a contest of individual wills. The support vehicles picked up more dropouts. Despite the ferocious cold, the piercing wind, the sun continued to radiate a thin glimmer of light. Ground blizzards, stirred by the gale, enveloped our bodies in ghostly funnels, knocking us off stride, nudging us toward the ditch. All faculties unrelated to the motor instinct of placing one foot in front of the other shut down completely. By late morning, those of us still in line were reduced to plodding automatons. The right side of my face, inadequately protected by the hood flap, felt as if it were vised between a pair of ruthless jaws. With each exhalation, tiny beads of ice bubbled across the surface of the bandanna, cloaking my lips and mouth.

At some point the Kyle water tower came into view, over a dreary copse of trees. The tower looked tantalizingly close. The more we walked, the more the tower seemed to diminish. Vehicles negotiating the road slowed to a crawl; the occupants stared pityingly out the windows. Two miles from Kyle, the road dipped along a creek bed, and for a little while, screened by a hedgerow of brown trees, we enjoyed a respite from the wind. Sherry Mattola dropped out. Pagan wobbled forward on rubbery legs. Head down, hunched over, George White Thunder remained in step with the Japanese. Bob Keyes was still in line, his face completely enveloped in the folds of a burnoose-like arrangement of flaps and scarves and tugged-up collars. A mere remnant of the original contingent finally tramped through the front door of the Little Wound School, five hours and ten grueling miles after starting out from Red Water Creek. Clothes sheeted with frost, eyes red-rimmed, cheeks prickly from the bite of the wind, we plodded like zombies into the cafeteria where the riders were already lined up at the counter to receive lunch. People turned to stare; the hubbub of conversation fell. A woman whose face I recognized but whose name I did not know came out from behind the counter bearing a long-handled spoon. Working the spoon like a riding quirt, she scattered the riders and support people and directed them to the back of the line. "Walkers!" she boomed in a hearty voice. "Let the walkers go to the head of the line! Move out of the way there! Step back! These walkers look half dead! Let's get 'em fed and warmed up! Hey, walkers! You walkers! Over here! Right here!"

An hour later we were off again—renewed, invigorated, thawed out, another load of buffalo soup sloshing in our bellies. Before departing from Kyle, we made a detour down a side street. In a grassless yard swept clean of snow, an old man—a full blood, with the bulbous nose and juicy eyes of a former alcoholic— waited with a lance. Bound near the top of the lance with thongs was a small hoop wrapped in rawhide. Two eagle feathers dangled from the tip. Above and below the hoop were twin circlets of fur. Dennis said something to the man and passed the lance to George White Thunder. The man nodded and twisted his glove-less hand as if making a signal. Dennis chuckled and shook a couple of cigarettes out of a pack, which the man accepted with a lopsided grin. George took the lead, and we marched in a ragged column back to the main road.

The wind that buffeted us that morning had mercifully died down. The road west out of Kyle rises in a straight line to a high point of sorts, before swerving to the left in an inclined arc toward the turnoff for Sharps Corner. The clement weather was no doubt responsible for the presence of so many walkers that afternoon. The atmosphere was festive. People paraded in clusters, yakking and smoking. An hour after leaving Kyle we reached the turnoff, but instead of striking out for Sharps Corner, we kept marching straight south toward the camp at Red Owl Springs. I was bothered by something. Since leaving Kyle, a man in an unmarked, shiny-new, navy blue Chevrolet pickup had played leapfrog with us, driving ahead and pulling off on the side, waiting for us to catch up, watching as we passed, then driving ahead again. The driver was white. He was hatless, with a balding skull offset by a bushy mustache. Each time we tromped past where he sat in the idling truck, he peered studiously at something tucked away in his lap—taking notes perhaps, consulting a book, a list? An old paranoia flared up through my chest. The third time the man pulled this caper, I eased up to where Dennis was walking with June-San.

"Hey, Dennis," I said. "The guy in the blue pickup over there. Any idea who he might be?"

"Who's that?"

"That guy. Right there."

The head of the line was approaching the pickup, which was backed into a driveway on the left side of the road.

Dennis kept his eyes straight ahead. "Could be an old friend of mine. There are a few around these days. I can't seem to get rid of them."

"FBI?"

Dennis was noncommittal. "Maybe. I don't know."

A memory from a long time ago came cartwheeling through my brain. November 1970, a massive anti-war rally was held in Washington, D.C. (the largest peacetime protest of its kind ever to assemble in the nation's capital); a well-behaved line of protestors marching single file made its way at a sluggish pace along a side street a block away from the White House. Each protestor carried a candle which he or she endeavored to keep from flickering out with a protective hat or cupped hand. A stiff cardboard placard lettered with the name of a dead American soldier dangled from the neck of each protestor. As we neared the corner of Pennsylvania Avenue a proctor with an identifying armband came down the line issuing a warning. "On the corner are two FBI guys with cameras. They're taking everyone's picture. Cover your face with a handkerchief if you want to protect your identity. If you don't give a shit, be sure and show them what you believe in."

Sure enough, at the corner, dressed in matching Robert Hall suits and streamlined ties—looking ridiculously conspicuous in contrast to the scruffy protestors—stood the two agents. As each protestor turned the corner onto Pennsylvania Avenue, heading toward the front gates of the White House, the agents aimed a camera and clicked the shutter; the pop of the flash (it was just getting dark) was accompanied by snarls and curses. Wisely the agents did not step too close. Just as I reached the corner, an agent approached with a black camera. The instant he snapped the shutter I threw my hand, index finger extended, in front of my face. "Fuck you, Jack!" I growled. A flash exploded to my left. The first guy was a decoy. The second guy, waiting by the curb, stepped forward and caught me flat-footed in a three-quarters profile with my right hand pronging in front of my nose. I turned like a wet cat, hissing and spitting, but the agent had already backed off.

"Let's stop here," Dennis said abruptly to June-San. "We need to pray."

He tugged at George White Thunder's coat and pointed toward a snow-crusted clearing across the road a few yards in advance of where the blue pickup was idling. When all the walkers were assembled, Pagan carried a coffee can of smoldering sage around the inside of the circle. Despite having broken his fast, Pagan still looked emaciated. His pale forehead, partially obscured by the visor of a beat-up cap, was prematurely furrowed with wrinkles. The sweet odor of balmy sage rippled through my nostrils. I sucked in a breath, hissed it out, and mouthed a wordless prayer.

"We got some more miles to go to the campsite at Red Owl Springs," Dennis said in a commanding voice which the guy in the pickup couldn't possibly miss, even with the window rolled up. "It's been a hard day. The spirits are with us. We are blessed by their presence. On top of that hill behind you, there's a white church." Everyone in the circle looked back over their shoulders or craned their necks. "In the graveyard out back lies the body of Frank Fools Crow. He spent his entire life helping the Oglala people. In 1973 he came to see us a number of times when we were besieged at Wounded Knee. His spirit is with us on this walk. I'd like a moment of silence to honor his memory . . ."

Fools Crow—thirteen times, under a flag of truce, as ceremonial leader of the Lakota Nation, the venerable elder passed through the cordon of FBI and federal marshals to make contact with the defenders holed up in their bunkers around the church and graveyard on top of the knoll overlooking Wounded Knee Creek; the same knoll where, on the evening of December 28, 1890, four Hotchkiss guns had been positioned with their barrels pointing toward Big Foot's camp. Fools Crow devoted his entire life to healing the wounds inflicted upon the Lakota people by atrocities such as Wounded Knee. He died in November of 1989, seven months shy of his one hundredth birthday. A traditional service was held in the gym of the Little Wound High School. The procession carrying his casket to the tiny church on the hill behind us stretched out for three-and-a-half miles. As hundreds of people looked on, pallbearers wearing feathered war bonnets covered the casket with a multicolored star quilt before lowering it into the ground.

Past the spot where we paused to pray, the blacktopped road changed to hard-packed dirt. The guy in the blue pickup elected not to tail us any further—at that point we were maybe four miles from Red Owl Springs. Evidently he had completed his inventory of possible subversives; I was relieved to see the pickup speeding back toward Kyle. A line of bluffs loomed along the western horizon, dimly silhouetted in the light of the declining sun. Thoughts of food tantalized my palate: chopped sirloin smothered in onions, mashed potatoes and gravy, niblets of yellow corn, strings of green beans. I plunged a fork into an imaginary plate just as a beat-up, four-door Chrysler at least two decades old, as wide as an army halftrack and making nearly as much noise, clattered toward us along the dirt road. Spotting the lance with the eagle feathers in George's hands, and then recognizing Dennis, the driver braked the battered car to a halt. Another man sat in the passenger seat; he was squat and heavy-set, with a plump face and flowing black hair that reached past his shoulders. As the head of the line neared the car, both doors suddenly swung wide; both men with a lurch of their heavy bodies lifted themselves out of their seats and stood up on the door frames, their round fleshy, hatless heads rising over the pocked and dented roof. Slowly, with a deliberate motion—as Dennis and the rest of us pulled even—the two men, as if on cue, without fanfare or histrionics, doubled their right hands into compact fists and raised their arms in the air. The wind seemed to pick up for a fraction of a second. As if by a whispered signal, the people at the head of the line quickened their step. Solemn and unsmiling, Dennis glanced over at the two men. His dark, hooded, deep-set eyes betrayed a flicker of recognition, which gradually mellowed into an expression of guarded pleasure. Up from his side in a careful movement he brought his long right arm, up past his ear, fingers balled, thumb clenched, elbow forming a stiff right angle. It was the first Red Power salute I'd seen on the entire trip. The two men perched in the doors of the dilapidated Chrysler held the salute until the entire line passed by.

Something else happened at the end of that long day. A member of the band of French riders, the *Amities Franco-Lakota*, had to drop out leaving a horse available, and Bo was asked if he wanted to ride the twenty-six-mile leg from Red Water Creek to Red Owl Springs. It took till midmorning to round up all the horses that had escaped from the corral the night before; that afternoon, after the wind died down and the temperature softened a few degrees, the riders made good time. The sun was poised to descend as they topped a hill overlooking the campsite. The support vehicles had already arrived; cook fires were spluttering, and several tipis had been thrown up. The riders fanned out in a long line across the brow of the hill, waiting in the glow of those final moments for Percy White Plume to herd the stragglers into place. Then, with everyone accounted for, with all the riders lined up stirrup to stirrup, with the horses pawing the ground, with the air hushed and still and breathless in the last effusion of light, Alex White Plume rose in the saddle and swung his arm. Slowly, to the creak of stiff leather, to the steady thunk of marching hooves, the entire line of two hundred riders converged on the camp.

"It was incredible," said Bo. "For me, it was the most magnificent moment of the trip. Nobody said a word. Nobody broke rank and ran ahead. Everything was as stately and measured as a symphonic beat. Together, rider to rider, like a mighty wave, we came down that hill. The women working the fires saw us coming and started ululating in high-pitched voices. Dogs barked. Men came running out of the tipis banging drums and shouting. We could have been a returning war party. For a few moments it was like what it must have been 150 years ago. The light from the fading sun was delicately soft. Not a breath of wind blew. The silhouettes of the trees against the pale sky were like inky drawings. Many of the riders were crying. I was shaking like a leaf. The solidarity, the togetherness, was overwhelming. It was the most fantastic moment of my life."

8

Suppose [I say] that it was an accident. Why should the soldiers have fired when no shots had been poured into them? Was there no authority and no discipline among the officers and soldiers? Could they not wait 'til the recalcitrant Indians, or Indians who forcibly refused to deliver their guns, were overcome or restrained? It is said Indians in the Council arose when the first shot occurred. Was it not natural that they should do so without intention to fight? The action of the troops was over hasty, premature and more like a mob than trained soldiery.

—*Eli Ricker,* The Ricker Tablets *(1907)*

Dewey Beard barely slept a wink that final night. A handsome, robust man in his late twenties, better known to his compatriots as Iron Hail, he was a seasoned hunter and warrior, a veteran (as a teenager) of the Little Big Horn battle. He was also married to a woman named Wears Eagle and was the father of a one-month-old boy. From the Cheyenne River encampment many miles to the north, he had traveled with Big Foot's entourage in the immediate company of his family: father, mother, wife, five brothers, a sister, and infant son. They were a close-knit family, affectionate and caring; the mood in the white soldiers' camp along Wounded Knee Creek the night of December 28 made them all restless and uneasy. The proximity of the troopers, the Hotchkiss guns perched on the knoll, the liquor that many of the officers had imbided, the refusal of the sentries to permit any adults to wander out of camp contributed to the disquieting feeling that something awful was about to happen.

Before the sun rose over the shallow valley carved out by the meandering creek, Dewey's father emerged from Big Foot's tent after conversing with the other headmen. His face was grave. Huddled with his family a few minutes later, he told them what he and the others had discussed in the starched white, wall-sided tent with its wood-burning stove which the military had provided to make Big Foot comfortable. "I will give you advice," he said. "They say it is peace but I am sure there is going to be fighting today. I have been in war all my life, and I know when my heart is growing bitter that there is going to be a fight. I have come to tell you—all my sons—what I want you to do. If one or two Indians go to start trouble first, I don't want you to go with them. If the white people start trouble first, then you can do what you want to—you can die among your own relations in defending them. All you, my dear sons, stand together and if you die at once among your relations defending them I will be satisfied. Try to die in front of your relations, the old folks and the little ones, and I will be satisfied if you die trying to help them. Don't get excited. When one or two under the Government laws start trouble they are arrested and taken into court and put in jail, but I don't want any of you to get into such trouble, but to stand back until all the whites assail us, and then defend our people. I have come to tell you this as advice before the trouble begins. I want you to heed my warnings."

A short time later the regimental bugler sounded reveille with a stuttery toot that brought everyone out of their tents and tipis into the cold, still air. On the army side, cook fires were heated up, coffee pots commenced to gurgle, slabs of biscuits and rashers of bacon were soon warming. Inside the Indian compound there was little activity. A few fires burned; people stood around, waiting. The best that any of the Miniconjous could hope for was that the army would not be too demanding in their business, and that before the sun was too high they would be on their way to Pine Ridge to join their Oglala cousins.

Sometime after sunup, a crier went from tipi to tipi in the Indian encampment, calling, "Come to council! Come to council!" Colonel James W. Forsyth, commander of the Seventh Cavalry, newly arrived from regimental headquarters at Pine Ridge, was under strict orders from his superior, General John Brooke, to disarm the Indians. Forsyth's job was to complete the task that Major Samuel Whitside had initiated the previous afternoon upon first encountering Big Foot's people, but which he had been dissuaded from doing by the strong objections of his mixed-blood interpreter, John Shangreau. What had failed, for whatever reason, to be implemented the day before would be implemented today without delay. That was the first order of business, the primary objective of the military unit that had drawn itself around the band of weary Indians in a threatening noose.

Colonel Forsyth was an officer of the old school: disciplined, by the book, unimaginative. He had commanded the Seventh Cavalry since 1886. He looked every inch the popular image of the senior officer: square chin, piercing eyes, bushy eyebrows, trim mustache, a leonine head of iron-gray hair. A string of Civil War brevets had culminated in the rank of major general of volunteers. Since 1865, however, he had had little command experience. In the 1876 war against the Lakota and Cheyenne, he had served on General Philip Sheridan's staff, first as an aide-de-camp, then as a military secretary. Other than a brief skirmish against the Bannocks in 1878, he had never led troops in battle against Indians.

The morning of December 29, 1890, Colonel Forsyth was not particularly disposed toward compromising or humoring Big Foot's band of Miniconjous. An order was an order; a dutiful officer, Forsyth had no intention of negotiating with these renegades in order to compel them to give up their arms. He would see to it that the order was obeyed. He was well aware of what had happened to Colonel Sumner when that officer had tried to indulge Big Foot and let the chief bring in his own band on his own terms. Fate had intervened in the form of the rumor-mongering Red Beard, and Big Foot had panicked and fled, and now, many miles southwest of the Cheyenne River, what should have been done up there would have to be done down here. Failure to relieve the Miniconjous of their weapons was a mistake that would not be repeated. The prestige of the army—the wounded pride of the Seventh Cavalry—was riding on Forsyth's epauleted shoulders.

Eight troops of cavalry were present that morning, 470 officers and men; in addition, there was a contingent of 30 Oglala scouts and a battery of four rapid-fire Hotchkiss cannons. Of the Indians there were possibly between 370 and 400; of these, perhaps 120 men and boys could be considered as possible combatants. Of the 120, how many were actually armed is impossible to determine. Though some 60 weapons were collected before violence broke out, there is no way of knowing how many additional pistols and rifles were concealed under the blankets the Indian men had draped around their shoulders. Even if the 120 potential warriors had been armed with pistols and rifles, they were no match for the 470 troopers, and they were certainly no match for the Hotchkiss guns poised on the knoll.

The order to disarm spelled disaster from the start. A lever-action Winchester rifle was a treasured possession of a Lakota warrior. He fed his family with it; it was his primary means of defense. Boxed in by hostile troops, ordered about by bearded officers, exhausted by the grueling march from the Cheyenne River, the Miniconjous were understandably edgy. They might cough up a few useless rifles, they might turn over a pistol or two, but their Winchesters and other prized weapons they intended to conceal under the blankets that drooped from their shoulders.

On a flat space in front of Big Foot's tent, the men and boys were assembled. Around them, ringing an oblong circle roughly sixty feet by a hundred feet, Colonel Forsyth ordered Troops K and B to form a guard line, with individual soldiers spaced from four to six feet apart. To the north of the ring stood the white tents of the cavalry encampment; to the west and south were the Miniconjou tipis, crowded with women and a few elders hastily packing up and readying themselves for the final leg of the journey to Pine Ridge. Playing around the tents, blissfully unaware of the drama unfolding a few yards away, were scores of children. Running along the south edge of the Indian camp was a ravine; several yards east of the agency road, the ravine broached onto

Wounded Knee Creek. The ravine was broad and deep, with steep sides and overhanging banks. On the far side of the ravine, saddled up in an orderly line, waiting patiently in the frigid air, were elements of Troops A and I.

Big Foot—desperately sick, bleeding from the nose—was helped out of the Sibley tent and propped up on the ground in front of the opening. Other elders took their places on either side of the moribund chief. Accounts vary as to what actually took place during the next two hours. Eli Ricker, a white rancher from Rushville, Nebraska, many years after the fact, took down voluminous personal testimonies from Lakota survivors, white soldiers, and mixed-blood witnesses. These accounts—confused and contradictory, harrowing and detailed—provide an indispensable source of primary material for anyone seeking to puzzle out how the fighting began, and why.

The council opened with Forsyth saying through interpreters Philip Wells and Little Bat Garnier that the Great Father in Washington had instructed him to confiscate all Miniconjou weapons. The colonel was careful to add that the owners would be adequately compensated. Once all the guns were secured, a wagon train and escort would be provided for the long haul back to the Cheyenne River. (Forsyth evidently said nothing about the Miniconjous going on to Pine Ridge and linking up with the Oglala.) To this overture several Indians nodded and said, "Good, very good."

Forsyth then ordered ten Indians from one end of the council and ten from the other to go into the tipi encampment and bring back all the weapons they could find. Those Indians chosen for this onerous duty reluctantly stood up and strolled between the cordon of guards and disappeared into the tipis. An hour elapsed before they drifted back, one by one, clutching armloads of antiquated rifles and revolvers. The weapons, totaling around sixty, were heaped in two piles at either end of the council; a special guard was posted at each pile.

When Forsyth saw the condition of the weapons, his patience wore thin. With some heat he said to Philip Wells, "You tell Big Foot that yesterday at the time of surrender his Indians were well armed, and that I am sure he is deceiving me."

The warriors who had searched the tipis insisted to their chief that no other guns were to be found. In a croaky whisper, Big Foot denied Colonel Forsyth's allegation. Forsyth called to Major Whitside, and the two officers conferred in urgent whispers.

Big Foot at this point was entangled in a difficult situation that demanded the best of his diplomatic skills; because of his illness, he was unable to exercise those skills. That he knew there were additional weapons concealed in the tipis and on the persons of some of the warriors there can be no doubt. Tension between the two sides was accelerating; the officers were showing their frustration; matters were moving toward a critical edge. Clearly, the offering of sixty weapons was not enough to satisfy the *wasicu*. Big Foot needed time, and time was running out. The tone of Colonel Forsyth's voice was harsh and abrupt. So close were the soldiers with their rifles at ready, they seemed to be standing in the Indians' faces. If someone in authority could have said, "Wait. Let's go slow with this. Let's take our time, and make sure no one gets needlessly upset," what followed might have been avoided. Had Colonel Sumner been in command, for example, he might have sat down with Big Foot and smoked awhile and exchanged a few pleasantries and given the ailing chief and his headmen time to soothe the ruffled feelings of their militant warriors. But Colonel Forsyth was in charge, and he wanted results from the order he had summarily delivered. He had a mission to complete, and he wasn't going to be satisfied until every weapon was taken into custody. Big Foot was in a terrible quandary. The hardening of attitudes on both sides was squeezing his dwindling reserve of options and energies into a smaller and smaller space. His heart must have sunk like a stone when he heard the colonel say, "Since you won't bring them yourselves, I will detail a squad of soldiers to search the tipis."

When this was translated into Lakota, the assembled warriors began to fidget and stir. Summoning up the last remnants of his dwindling strength, Big Foot tried, without much success, to reassure his people that everything would be all right.

Two details, one led by Captain Charles Varnum, the other by Captain George Wallace, commenced to go in a systematic fashion from tipi to tipi. They confiscated anything remotely resembling a weapon: knives, axes, hatchets, bows and arrows, even eating implements. They searched under blankets and piles of clothing; they peered behind tent flaps; they frisked women and old men, lifting them bodily off the ground; they unpacked wagons, already packed for the final ride to Pine Ridge, and searched through their contents. Captain Wallace, a popular commander, spoke calmly to the people and urged his men to be mannerly. He touched children under the chins and tousled their hair. Somewhere along the way, he picked up a stone war club, which he tapped gingerly against his leg.

Meanwhile, back in the council circle, an incident occurred, which, though denied by some, was later attested to in the Ricker interviews by two of the most reliable Indian informants, Dewey Beard and his brother Joseph Horn Cloud. According to them, soldiers in the guard surrounding the council were instructed by their officers to point their single-shot Springfield rifles at the foreheads of certain Indians and click the hammers against the empty chambers. Reportedly, the purpose of this fiendish charade was to punish the Indians for failing to relinquish their weapons to Major Whitside the day before. The effect on the Indians was disruptive. Rumblings arose from their ranks, bitter vocal protests. "Take courage! Take courage!" they cried. "We are not children to be talked to like this! We are a people in this world!"

Adding to the restiveness were the antics of a holy man, whose name most likely was Yellow Bird and who, at the west end of the circle, commenced to hold up both hands and pray in a supplicating voice. Yellow Bird's body from head to toes was coated with blue paint; yellow spots the size of silver dollars spangled his skin. Despite the cold, he wore only leggings, a breechcloth, and a headdress. Slowly, then with mounting enthusiasm, he commenced to shuffle back and forth, singing in a ragged, high-pitched voice.

Colonel Forsyth immediately took notice. "What is that man saying?" he asked Philip Wells.

Wells needed no prompting. His own curiosity was aroused. He walked over to the west end of the circle. When Forsyth called to him again, he waved his hand impatiently. "Don't disturb me, Colonel. I must pay close attention to catch all he means. I will let you know just as soon as he says something you should know."

One can only imagine Forsyth's dilemma at this moment. The Indians had refused to surrender their best weapons. The menacing presence of the soldiers, coupled with the exhortations of the strange holy man, caused the Miniconjous to become more agitated. Many of the younger warriors inside the circle had pulled their blankets over their heads, leaving one eye visible, a traditional gesture of irritation and anger. Had Forsyth been more experienced, he might have tried to ease the situation by calling off the search and ordering an extra helping of rations. Instead, he did nothing. "All right," he called gruffly to his interpreter, and walked off.

Part Santee Sioux, born on the Minnesota frontier in 1850, Philip Wells had both fraternized with Indians and fought against them. According to witnesses, that morning at Wounded Knee he displayed the unpleasant tendency of the mixed blood to behave in a high-handed manner toward full bloods; a loquacious man, Wells spoke condescendingly to people he regarded as inferior. Instead of softening and soothing the tone of Forsyth's curt orders, Wells translated them verbatim, adding his own harsh emphasis, which contributed to the Indians' discomfort.

By now Yellow Bird was stooping over, snatching up handfuls of powdery dust, casting the dust in a circular motion toward the soldiers and over the heads of his own people. Around in a circle he gyrated, muttering and gesticulating. Wells edged closer. "Ha-ha! Ha-ha!" he heard Yellow Bird declare. "I have lived long enough!" Turning toward the young men gathered at the west end of the ring, Yellow Bird counseled them not to be afraid but to make their hearts strong for what was about to occur. "There are many soldiers here," he cried, "but they cannot harm you. Their bullets will not go toward you, but will pass over the prairie. If they do go toward you, they will not penetrate you. As you just saw me throw up the dust and it floated away, so will the soldiers' bullets float away harmlessly over the prairie."

Wells was becoming more alarmed by the moment. Sensing

something was awry, Colonel Forsyth called out to the interpreter, "You'd better get out of there. It's starting to look dangerous."

"In a minute, Colonel. I want to see if I cannot get this fellow to quiet them."

The "fellow" Wells referred to was Big Foot's brother or brother-in-law (his exact identity is not clear). "Friend," Wells said softly, "go in among the young men and quiet them and talk to them as an elder should."

In an exaggerated voice Big Foot's brother replied, "Why, friend, your heart seems to beat! Who's talking of trouble or fighting?"

"Yes, friend," Wells retorted, "my heart beats when I see so many helpless women and children if anything should happen."

"Friend, it is unpleasant that your heart should even beat."

The tension among the soldiers was intensifying by the second. They were young, and they were woefully inexperienced; at the moment their officers were not doing a very good job of either calming their fears or controlling the situation inside the circle. A force had been set in motion that no one present seemed to know how to deflect or defuse. Perhaps a veteran junior officer such as Captain George Wallace (commander of K Troop) could have staved off the impending disaster, but the hierarchy of command was inflexible, and the tone for the morning's activity had been irreversibly set by Colonel Forsyth; disarming the Miniconjous was his show, and he was determined to push it through to a conclusion. If ever there was a moment in American military history when the rigidity of the command structure needed to be challenged, it was on the morning of December 29, 1890, along the banks of Wounded Knee Creek. But no challenge was forthcoming, not from the junior officers and certainly not from the enlisted men. (Philip Wells, an outsider, part Indian, might have provided that challenge, similar to the manner in which John Shangreau the previous day had talked Major Whitside out of disarming the Miniconjous, but he failed to take the initiative.) Cold, uncomfortable, insecure, the soldiers were becoming demoralized. Their confidence was questionable, their discipline suspect. The most notable success the majority had achieved since joining the army was learning how to ride a horse. They knew how to handle their single-shot, breech-loading rifles, and they knew they belonged to an outfit that in 1876 had suffered one of the worst defeats in the three-hundred-year history of warfare against the North American aborigines. They knew from the stories they'd heard from the veterans, as well as from the dime novels and newspapers they'd read, that the Lakota were a treacherous lot of savages. Directly in front of them, milling restlessly about, urged on by a fantastic blue-daubed figure, were over a hundred sullen and hostile specimens of a race whose manner of behavior was inscrutable, and whose customs and dress were grotesque.

Meanwhile, the two squads detailed by Colonel Forsyth to search the tipis weren't having much luck. They were thorough in their inspection, and managed to turn up a few knives, a few utensils, but disappointingly few pistols or rifles. The spectacle of the troopers combing methodically through the encampment contributed to the general feeling of unease. Despite Captain Wallace's admonitions, some of the soldiers did not behave as professionally as they should have. Their actions were clumsy and rude; they made insulting remarks. Cries of protest from the women greeted their boorish behavior; the entire camp was soon in an uproar.

It was about this time that a tall, powerfully built man stepped out from the crowd of Indians at the west end of the ring and started to stalk Philip Wells. The interpreter, his nerve endings atingle, noticed the man right away. Each time the Indian tried to slip behind him, Wells turned his body to keep the man in full view. Clutching the barrel of his rifle with both hands, Wells planted the butt on the ground and pivoted around the fixed point in an awkward pirouette.

By now the tension inside the circle was approaching the combustion point. As if sensing something, Captain Wallace sidled up to Joseph Horn Cloud, who spoke English. Years later, speaking to Eli Ricker, Joseph Horn Cloud clearly remembered Captain Wallace's fateful words. "Joseph," he murmured, "you better go over to the women and tell them to let the wagons go and saddle up their horses and be ready to skip. There's going to be trouble."

Joseph did as he was advised. When the soldiers of K troop on the south side of the circle refused to let him through, Captain Wallace indicated it was okay. Joseph slipped out of the circle and disappeared between the tipis.

Meanwhile, Yellow Bird was so vocal he attracted Colonel Forsyth's attention again. "What is that man saying?" he called to Wells.

"Sir, I fear he is making mischief."

"Then tell him to sit down."

Wells did, and after a few more gyrations, Yellow Bird plunked himself down. He continued to sing and pray and urge the young men on. He scooped up more handfuls of dust and threw them over his head and let them seep between his fingers. *Wasicu* eyewitnesses insist that the act of releasing the dirt was a signal to the Indians to open fire, but such an assertion defies comprehension and even good sense. Granted, the warriors in the circle had been riled up by Yellow Bird's utterances and the bumptious attitude of the soldiers, but to initiate a point-blank shootout with so many women and children nearby was suicidal. The Lakota did not engage in warfare in such a reckless and fool-hardy fashion. If Big Foot or any member of his party had enter-tained a notion to grapple with the soldiers, they would have done so the previous afternoon upon first encountering Major Whitside's command, where the terrain was more favorable for defense, where there was a clear avenue of escape, and where pro-tecting the women and children was easier to achieve.

Frustrated by the results of the search of the Indian camp, Colonel Forsyth played his trump card. With Philip Wells trans-lating, he announced that each warrior in the council circle would have to submit to an inspection. He did not like having to do this, he said, but he had no choice. Each man would have to come forward, remove his blanket, and deposit any concealed weapons on the ground.

About twenty older men responded. They stood up and ambled toward the Colonel, who stood a few feet from Big Foot's tent. One by one, the men pulled off their blankets and passed between Major Whitside and Captain Varnum. The search of the old men revealed no weapons. Grudgingly, in sullen groups, the younger men lined up to pass between the officers. Three rifles, one a Winchester, and a quantity of ammunition were found on the first three. The tension inside the circle intensified. Yellow Bird, still seated, commenced to harangue the warriors in the circle, all the while scooping up handfuls of dust and trailing them between his fingers. Lieutenant James D. Mann, out in front of K Troop in the absence of Captain Wallace who was searching the last few tipis, said later, "I had a peculiar feeling come over me, some presentiment of trouble." Turning to his men, he said in a low voice, "Be ready. There is going to be trouble."

Accounts vary as to the precise incident that provoked the flash point that plunged this troubled scene into the melee that followed. Philip Wells in his testimony to Eli Ricker contends it was the Indians who fired the first shots. Charles Cressey, a reporter for the *Omaha Daily Bee*, supports this assertion. The majority of both Indian and *wasicu* survivors and eyewitnesses disagree. The consensus among them seems to be that, whatever the catalyst, it was accidental; a gun that went off somewhere in the assembled ranks provided the spark for the subsequent mayhem. Dewey Beard describes how a deaf Indian named Black Coyote refused to give up his rifle; he was having difficulty understanding why the Miniconjous were being asked to give up their weapons in the first place. It was winter. Food was scarce. Each warrior needed a weapon to help feed his family. A few Indians close to Black Coyote agreed that they would take it upon themselves to explain to the deaf man through sign language why the soldiers wanted his weapon. The Indians were confident that once they explained the situation, Black Coyote would hand over the rifle. But before they could try, several soldiers came up behind the deaf man and tried to wrest the gun away. There was a struggle. Black Coyote refused to yield. "Look out! Look out!" cried a soldier, who stepped back and leveled his gun. The rifle, held rigidly by Black Coyote in an upright position with the barrel pointed harmlessly in the air, accidentally discharged. A single shot splintered the gloomy air. The sound was like a clarion. The strain of the morning hours suddenly dissolved in a paroxysm of violence. Several Indians threw off their blankets and brought their weapons into play. The eruption of gunfire on both sides in some instances was simultaneous. With no audible order from their officers, soldiers of Troops K and B started blasting. "We were told by Colonel Forsyth to open up at the first sound of gunfire," an anonymous sergeant later confessed to Eli Ricker. "Fire rolled out simultaneously from all other units. I had a strange sickening feeling. I knew something dreadful was being done."

Boxed in at close quarters, the Miniconjous sitting in council or looking on were prominent targets. One of the first to die was Big Foot. When the firing began, he was supine, propped up on one shaky elbow. He raised up, only to be shot just below the neck simultaneously by both an enlisted man and an officer. (To this day the Lakota insist the U.S. Army maintained a "hit list" of troublesome leaders to be eliminated when the opportunity presented itself. The killing of Big Foot a few moments after the outbreak of gunfire seems to indicate as much; like Sitting Bull, he appears to have been targeted for assassination once violence broke out.) Big Foot's daughter, standing next to the tent in which her father had spent the night, dashed forward to aid the stricken man. A second bullet fired by the same officer pierced her between the shoulder blades, and she dropped to the ground.

For Philip Wells, the world literally exploded in his face. The Indian who'd been stalking him pulled a long, well-honed cheese knife from under his blanket; clutching the handle with both hands, he raised it over his head and drove it like a spike toward the interpreter's face. Wells fell to one knee; bracing the rifle over his head with both hands, he blocked the thrust and prevented the knife from drilling into his forehead. Unfortunately, the tip of the sharp blade gashed the top of his nose, nearly severing the nose from his face. To evade the shot he knew must come, the warrior dropped to his hands and knees. Wells waited an extra second before firing. The bullet punched into the man's side below the arm, and he pitched forward onto his face. A corporal ran up and pumped a slug into the Indian's back. With a deafening roar, the council circle was suddenly filled with screams and cries and whining bullets. No sooner had he delivered the *coup de grâce* to Wells's assailant than the corporal was struck down by a random shot from a soldier standing across the way.

With his nose dangling from his face by a few fleshy threads, Wells staggered away from the shooting. Behind the cordon, crazed with shock, he tried to rip the nose off his face. An officer shouted, "My God, man! Don't do that! That can be saved!" Taking Wells by the arm, he led him to the safety of some wagons. Inside the council circle, the firing intensified to a deadly crescendo. One of the first soldiers slain was Captain Wallace. Still carrying the stone club, he had just returned to his station in front of K Troop when a bullet blew away the top of his head.

Inside the circle, with soldiers firing at point-blank range, with those few Indians possessing weapons firing back as fast as they could, it was utter pandemonium. Dewey Beard was standing close to Big Foot and his own father when the shooting began. Around him, Indians reeled and dropped to the ground, crying out and kicking their legs. Dewey ran toward the soldiers of B Troop, guided in the swirl and confusion by the brass buttons of their uniforms which flashed through the acrid smoke like pinpoints of light. The barrel of a trooper's rifle discharged close to his ear, temporarily deafening him. Dewey grabbed the barrel and wrenched the rifle out of the soldier's hands; drawing his knife, he plunged it into the soldier's chest. The soldier groaned and seized Dewey by the throat; Dewey stabbed him in the side close to the heart. Moaning and flailing, the man went down; Dewey straddled his fallen body and stabbed him repeatedly in the kidneys till the man lay still.

On his feet, clutching the rifle, Dewey dashed for the ravine. A bullet struck his arm. He fell, rolled over, and bounded back on his feet. A soldier rose in front of him. Dewey pressed the trigger but the rifle was empty. The soldier aimed his rifle, but it failed to go off. In pain, stuffing a fresh bullet into the chamber, Dewey staggered between tipis, past screaming women and squalling children, past the bodies of dead and dying Indians. Another soldier popped up from nowhere. Dewey shot him in the chest. The impact toppled the soldier over backwards, where he writhed with agony. Dewey leaped over his flailing legs and plunged into the ravine. A bullet crunched him in the groin, sending him sprawling. Stunned, wounded now in two places, he pulled himself up to a sitting position. He reloaded and fired at the soldiers running toward the edge of the ravine. He managed to get off several rounds before a bullet splintered the rifle in his hands. Dewey threw the weapon away and limped to the bottom of the ravine.

A critical moment had been reached in the fight. The bloodshed of these first few minutes had been terrible; what followed would be even worse. Had the Seventh Cavalry officers and noncoms kept their heads and taken control and ordered their men to cease firing and fall back, the outcome of the morning's events might have been different. Hemmed in by the ravine and the Indian encampment, there was precious little space for Troops K and B to withdraw to; Colonel Forsyth had positioned his men not only where they could inflict casualties on one another in a deadly cross-fire but where they could not adequately retreat should Indian fire inside the council circle prove too damaging for them to hold their formation.

The majority of Indians who survived the initial volleys raced for the protection of the ravine and, armed with whatever weapons they already possessed or could pick up along the way, began potshotting back at the soldiers, at times with accuracy but with no sustained or concentrated pattern. In the best of all possible circumstances, the soldiers might have withdrawn to a safe distance and after a suitable interval opened negotiations through an interpreter, which might have led eventually to the Indians' surrender or at least to a cessation of hostilities. But nothing of the sort happened. Competent officers like Captain Wallace were dead. Nothing was heard from Colonel Forsyth. (As soon as firing broke out, he ran to the top of the knoll to obtain a better picture of what was going on.)

Something hideously awful had been released by the outbreak of violence. The reasons were many, and they were deeply embedded in the hateful attitude toward native people that had evolved over four hundred years of colonization and conquest. What followed on the tragic field at Wounded Knee after the first exchange of fire was little more than the massacre of innocents. It was as if that first shot had uncorked a pent-up reservoir of deep frustration and rage which could not be recapped, not by the power of any authority. The inexperience of the enlisted men has already been mentioned, and the fact that the majority were foreign-born and prejudiced toward Indians; the eruption of gunfire that winter morning marked the first combat that most of them had ever experienced. What also must be remembered is that six of the eight troop commanders of the Seventh Cavalry had served with the regiment since the Custer era; all but one of those commanders were survivors of the fighting along the Little Big Horn. The Seventh Cavalry bore the stigma of a special defeat that must have rankled many of its veterans in the most personal way. Vengeance is not a motive to be lightly dismissed for what took place at Wounded Knee. The fact that practically all vestiges of military discipline broke down in the chaos that followed is indicative that personal and racial vendettas were permitted to take precedence over professional standards and responsibilities. What had been an instinctive response to violence out of self-preservation in the opening moments changed to something more akin to outright murder. It is only natural that people being fired on will continue to fire back until the enemy is silenced. Professional soldiers, however, should be capable of modifying their tactics, even under the strain of hostile fire. According to witnesses, the initial fusillade of bullets lasted between five and ten minutes. What followed was, in some instances, a systematic campaign of extermination against those Indians—male, female, and child—who by some miracle had survived the first blasts and who were fleeing desperately for their lives.

On top of the knoll, Light Battery E, First U.S. Artillery, under the command of Captain Allyn Capron, held their fire until the last Indian had disappeared into the tipi encampment. Then, with little chance of harming their own men, the battery of four cannon went to work, raining shells down onto the camp, raking it from end to end. Presumably, the reason for firing into an area filled mostly with women, children, and old people was to flush out those men and boys—combatants such as Dewey Beard—who had fled there after the opening shots. Presumably, too, because of the heavy winter clothing most Miniconjous were wearing, it was difficult for the gunners (or soldiers down on the flat) to distinguish between males and females. (Children, because of their size, were a different story.) For whatever reason, from that elevation, peering down on the confusion, with the tents and tipis presenting prominent targets, the gunners wreaked a terrible havoc. When operated by a trained crew, the slim, elegant, breech-loading Hotchkiss could be fired fifty times a minute. (The Hotchkiss must not be mistaken for a primitive machine gun; Gatling guns were not used by the U.S. Army at Wounded Knee.) The shell weighed two pounds and ten ounces; it exploded on contact, spraying white-hot shrapnel in a deadly arc. Moments after the order had been given by Captain Capron, the Miniconjou encampment was shredded by high explosives. As the shells plowed into the tipis, peppering the Indians with fragments, they ran screaming in every direction. Those who weren't ripped apart became targets for the soldiers crowding the periphery. Earlier, when Joseph Horn Cloud had passed the word from Captain Wallace that trouble was about to break out, many families had saddled their horses and hitched up their teams. A lucky few managed to escape; the majority were cut down by the guns. A man and woman clinging to a bouncing horse were blown to bits by a direct hit. At one point, clambering out of the ravine, a team of two horses carrying three passengers with two men running frantically alongside whipping the horses with all their strength was spotted by Lieutenant Harry Hawthorne. "Can't you stop them?" he called to Corporal Paul Weinert. Weinert sighted the cannon and yanked the lanyard. With an accuracy that later was to earn the corporal the Medal of Honor, the shell blasted the wagon, horses, and Indians to bloody tatters. "It looked as if a pile of rags had been thrown into the air," Lieutenant Hawthorne later remarked.

Some of the personal encounters were ferocious beyond description. One woman, half-crazed by the severity of her wounds, crawled on her belly to a gut-shot soldier lying on his back. Clamped between her teeth was a butcher knife. As the soldier groveled with pain, the woman tilted herself up on her knees and, with the last of her strength, drove the knife into his chest. Another soldier dashed up and shot the woman in the head.

Taking advantage of the confusion, Yellow Bird fled into a tipi at the edge of the encampment. Through a slit in the canvas, he began squeezing off shots. A young soldier, brandishing a knife, vowing "to kill the son-of-a-bitch," charged the tipi. A bullet caught him in the stomach; with a strangled cry he crumpled to the ground. Enraged, the men of K Troop riddled the tipi with bullets. Undaunted, Yellow Bird fired back. The troopers rolled a hay bale up to the canvas and torched it. Flames crackled to the top of the lodgepoles; the smoke was suffocating. The tipi melted away, revealing the charred remains of Yellow Bird clad in a ghost shirt with cabalic designs that clung to his body like a scorched wrapper.

Reaching the bottom of the ravine, wounded in two places, Dewey Beard saw many children strewn about, struck by bullets fired by the soldiers on the rim. His rage was such that, as he later told Eli Ricker, even if he ate one of the soldiers, it would not appease his anger. From an old man he obtained another rifle. Accompanied by two other warriors, he charged the soldiers on the south side of the ravine, only to be driven back by gun blasts. Amidst the chaos, the screams, the zing of bullets cutting the air, almost as if by a miracle, Dewey encountered his mother (his father was already dead). Mortally wounded, staggering along the bottom of the ravine, swinging a revolver in her hand, she called out to her son, "Pass by me. I am going to fall down now." A hail of shots from both sides of the ravine ripped into her body. Pivoting back and forth, working the rifle as fast as he could reload, Dewey tried to defend her, but she was down and already dead. Like a blind man groping for the exit to a burning house, he lurched on down the ravine.

An old man drenched with blood thrust a lever-action Winchester in his hands. Dewey was too severely wounded in the right arm to manipulate the weapon with any success. The arm flopped uselessly at his side; clamping the thumb between his teeth, hunched over, the Winchester banging against his left shoulder, he ran along the ravine calling out to those still standing, "Take courage! Take courage!" Dead and dying Indians lay everywhere. More soldiers crowded to the edge of the ravine, pouring fire into its depths. Hugging the banks, women tore frantically at the frozen dirt, digging tiny pits in which to conceal their children. "It was now in the ravine just like a prairie fire when it reaches brush and tall grass and rages with new power," wrote Eli Ricker in 1907. "It was like hail coming down; an awful fire was concentrated on them now and nothing could be seen for the smoke."

By sheer chance, Dewey found his brother William Horn Cloud leaning against the bank, not far from the rim. He had been shot through the chest. His pain-crimped lips bubbled with blood as he tried to speak to his brother. With the aid of another Indian, Dewey carried the wounded man to the bottom of the ravine and tried to comfort him. (William Horn Cloud would die that evening from his wounds.) "Shake hands with me," he gasped. "I am dizzy now."

"Take courage," Dewey cried. "Our father told us it is better that all of us should die together than we should die separately at different times."

West along the ravine a few score yards, at an angle where the ravine turned abruptly south, there was a pocket of protection formed by an overhanging bank toward which those Indians still able to move now made their way. Dewey and others took cover and sent back sporadic fire, both toward the soldiers converging on the rim and up toward the top of the knoll. One of the bullets fired from under this protective eave struck Lieutenant Harry Hawthorne in the watch pocket of his uniform jacket, opening a wound and splattering watch parts deep into his abdomen. "I'll make them pay for that," growled Corporal Weinert. Calling to his crew, he pushed the light cannon by hand on its high wheels down the slope practically to the edge of the ravine. The shells, fired at point-blank range, pulverized the dirt overhang, collapsing it on top of the Miniconjous. Any chance they might have had to establish a defensive position was lost. "Now there went up from these dying people a medley of death songs that would make the hardest heart weep," wrote Eli Ricker. The crumbling overhang exposed the helpless Indians to intense fire. The carnage was appalling. A bullet whining past Dewey's head struck a woman in the back. Seemingly oblivious of the wound, she laughed out loud; her face lit up; she fell to her knees and died. A man armed with a bow and a fistful of arrows doubled over in front of her. A direct hit from Corporal Weinert's Hotchkiss gun tore a gaping hole in the stomach of another man. His hands described two faint circles before he keeled over on the ground.

Thinking of his own wife and infant son (barely a month old), Dewey struggled back up the ravine to locate them. (His wife was already dead; the boy was later found alive, still nursing at his mother's breast.) He came upon a band of women and children huddled in a shallow pit; they were all wounded; they were all being fired on by the soldiers. Levering the Winchester as best he could, he fired back, killing two soldiers (including an officer) and wounding others. The smoke and swirling haze prevented him from scoring additional hits. Bullets popped against the hard ground. At the impact of a cannon shell, the air seemed to shatter into a thousand pieces. Blind with pain, Dewey scrambled out of the ravine at a place where there were no soldiers. Limping, bleeding, he hobbled over a stretch of flat ground. Out of the smoke appeared his brother Joseph (whom Captain Wallace had warned of impending danger and who had left the encampment before fighting broke out). Joseph helped the wounded man onto a horse and led him away to safety.

With the pocket collapsed and no gunfire coming from it, Philip Wells, his nose bobbing from his ruined face like a cork from a string, started up the ravine calling out in Lakota, "All of you who are still alive, get up and come on over! You will not be molested or shot any more!"

Reluctantly, fearfully, their bodies twitching, death songs still spiraling from their constricted throats, those Indians who could walk or crawl crept toward the rim. Several soldiers went down to assist the seriously wounded. Farther along the ravine, a badly wounded Indian trying to push himself off the ground with both hands was mowed down in a burst of fire from members of E Troop who were advancing along the ravine from the northwest.

As the gunfire faded, Colonel Forsyth walked stiffly down from the top of the knoll. Dazed and confused, he surveyed the wreckage of the once peaceful camp. Under the dark blue rim of his gold-braided hat, his face was stricken and pale. As more shots echoed up and down the ravine, the steely composure that masked his distinguished features melted away. "Stop it!" he screamed, his voice ringing like a harsh chime in the winter air. "For God's sake, stop shooting at them!"

9

Sioux and elephants never forget.

—*Mary Crow Dog,* Lakota Woman *(1990)*

It was barely light when we reached Sharps Corner, but someone had started a fire, and the walkers were already huddled
around the flames, warming their hands and stamping their feet.
The sky was a lumpy gray, drab and colorless, heavy with the
promise of unpleasant weather. The Japanese had boiled a pot of
tea and were passing their cups to people who had none. Around
the fire there was the sleepy rumble of small talk, though the
rumble soon sputtered out into a contemplative silence broken
only by the crackle of burning logs.

The cold was savage. It penetrated coats, sweaters, boot lin-
ers, thermal underwear; it penetrated the pimply flesh of the
people huddled around the fire with the sharp edge of a steel
knife. June-San was the only person not wrapped to the eyeballs
in warm clothing. She wore a green wool cap. Her alert eyes glittered through the lenses of her wire-frame glasses. The rest of us,
including the Japanese, stood around like a bunch of bowling
pins, staring into the fire, trying with the force of our eyes to
siphon off a little warmth, to dispense that warmth like a fluid
to every part of our bodies. A brilliant, multicolored quilt draped
the form of a middle-aged Lakota woman standing next to
June-San. The woman stood out against the monochrome backdrop like a tropical blossom. Her wide-boned face was pinched
and constricted. She held herself delicately, as if fearful that her
body might crack. She looked as if she'd been lifted out of a dis-

turbing dream and transported to this tiny crossroads hamlet deep inside the Pine Ridge Reservation to continue her sleep standing up in front of the snapping fire.

From Sharps Corner to Wounded Knee was twelve miles. There were many snow-glazed hills to climb, many wind-sliced ridge tops to crawl over before the road swung down into the spacious, shallow bowl of Wounded Knee Creek. Today would be the final test of our resolve. Today, on the swell of an imponderable emotion, we would finally arrive at our destination. Already the cold burned through my clothing like a corrosive acid. Someone heard on the radio that the temperature was thirty below, with the forecast indicating that, for the rest of the day, thirty below was about as warm as it would get. Something that Jim Garrett, one of the *Sitanka Wokiksuye* organizers, had said earlier in the week echoed through my head: "We Lakota believe that we come into this world with nothing but our bodies. The only way we can demonstrate our sincerity to *Wakan Tanka* is through the intensity of our suffering. That's why we hang from ropes during the sun dance. That's why we cry out for a vision in the loneliness of the *hanblechya*. And that's why we're here today, walking and riding through this terrible cold."

That final morning around the fire at Sharps Corner, Dennis Banks blessed the precious warmth of the crackling flames with a pinch of tobacco; then he passed a coffee can full of smoldering sage around the circle; we fanned its smoke across our chests and arms and faces to purify ourselves for the ordeal ahead. The sage smelled sweet and lingered fragrantly in our nostrils. Dennis flipped his cigarette into the fire and grasped the lance in his right hand. "When we come into Wounded Knee this afternoon, we'll be exhausted and sore, but I want us to look proud; I want us to look strong."

His voice rang through the icy air. The broad features of his bearded face appeared to have been chiseled out of a slab of stone. There was a stolidity to his presence that, apart from his well-know name, added a note of gravity to our endeavors.

"We've come a long way together, and we've got another hard day ahead of us. When we march down that hill this afternoon, I want us to hold our heads high. There'll be TV and media. There'll be lots of young people and elders watching, and I want them to know that our hearts are full of courage and hope. What we are doing here can give strength to people everywhere. Big Foot's band did not die in vain a hundred years ago. We are celebrating their memory; we are marking their suffering with a sacrifice of our own. Their spirits are with us now. Their spirits will be with us this afternoon when we walk into Wounded Knee."

June-San drew the prayer drum out of the scabbard looped to her shoulder. The Japanese filled their cylindrical bottles with hot tea and tightened their zippers and adjusted the straps of their day packs. The Lakota woman pulled the colorful quilt closer around her shoulders. There was a reluctance on the part of everyone to leave the comfort of the fire. The cold was so fierce that when I took off my glove to jot down a note, my fingers cramped with pain.

Dennis handed the fur-ringed lance to George White Thunder. George held the lance away from his body, as if its powers were too formidable to bring in close. George wore his quilted blue coat and navy blue watch cap, with the eagle feather drooping to his shoulder. The expression on his prematurely aged face was melancholy and unsmiling. The little muscles below his puffy eyes were bunched into tight knots.

"Lead the way," said Dennis. One by one, holding out our hands to catch the last flicker of warmth, we backed away from the fire, George in front. Trailing one another in a long, snow-crunching line, we circled the fire in a clockwise direction. Our circle had dissolved, but only momentarily; up the road, along the way, it would link up again, and we would partake of its energy and comfort. But first we had to brave the cold. With June-San tapping the drum, with the stirring baritone of Shonosuke Ohkura lifting in prayer through the dawn air, we started single file along the road.

The previous evening, amidst a babble of voices and the thunk of basketballs, as Dana, Bo, Bob Keyes, and I lolled on our pallets on the gym floor of the Little Wound School, Russell Means made a slow, dignified circuit of the court to announce in a steady voice that, for anyone interested, there would be an AIM meeting in the lunchroom in ten minutes. Russell Means can polarize a crowd of Indians quicker than a magnet can separate iron particles. Those Indians opposed to the meeting stared scornfully at those who wandered into the lunchroom. By the time we arrived, Russell was in full throat, blasting South Dakota governor George Mickelson's feeble efforts to promote "reconciliation" between Indians and whites; he then ripped into the franchise food business in Rapid City, criticizing it for failing to hire a sufficient number of minorities.

The contents of the speech were familiar to anyone who had followed the fortunes of the American Indian Movement for the past twenty years; the delivery was also familiar, blustery and confrontational. Russell's oratorical technique was vintage 1960s, direct and challenging; he presented himself as the primary target, the personal embodiment of a host of outraged wrongs. Sturdy and defiant, he stood in the center of the lunchroom floor, his arms folded across his chest, his jaw pugnaciously outthrust. Facing him in a ragged assembly of stiff plastic chairs were maybe fifty listeners, a number of whom were bearded *wasicu* from Europe. The warrior voice was confident and fully amplified; the delivery, however, seemed more performance than substance, as if he were lip-synching a familiar tape that everyone had heard, but that everyone, for old-time's sake, had come to hear again.

Dennis spoke next. Other than bringing up the Black Hills issue again (as he had around the council fire on Christmas Eve), he avoided anything with a hard edge. Mostly he was funny and anecdotal. Before coming to Pine Ridge in the 1970s, he had spent a night or two in jails in Minneapolis and Wisconsin; as a result of agitating for Indian rights in South Dakota, he had been charged with crimes and felonies amounting to 250 years of possible imprisonment. "Russell told me that life was tough out here, that South Dakota was a racist state, and, by God, he was right. I just want to finish the work we started so I can go back to Wisconsin where I won't be treated so badly."

The laughter greeting this remark was genuine. Dennis was a street coyote, shifty and elusive. Unlike Russell's self-righteous assaults, Dennis's pitch was humorous and shot full of self-deprecating asides. Swaying his broad shoulders, leaning into his words with rhythmic emphasis, he shifted from foot to foot like a boxer. The crowd warmed to his stories as it didn't to Russell's fulminations, and the space inside the lunchroom rang loudly with appreciative snorts and chortles. Despite the familiarity of their respective deliveries, it was a pleasure to watch the two do what they do best: captivate a crowd, rile emotions, challenge complacency. That evening they reminded me of a popular '60s rock group—stouter, less nimble, a bit creaky in the joints—reprising a performance that had once garnered them notoriety and fame.

It took two hours to walk to the tiny hamlet of Porcupine. The swirling wind tormented the line of toiling walkers. By nine o'clock the sky wasn't much lighter than it had been at dawn; a solid mass of clouds glowered down to the treetops. Snow fell in idle clusters, but it seemed too cold to snow to any serious extent; it was the cold we had to contend with.

In Porcupine we were ushered into a recreation hall decorated with murals depicting the exploits of notable Oglala warriors. The high-ceilinged interior was comfortable and warm; we sat on wooden benches and drank fresh coffee and bit by bit thawed out. The final leg of the road from Sharps Corner had followed the route of Porcupine Creek; for the final mile or two we were sheltered from the wind by a line of sculpted bluffs paralleling both sides of the road. There was little conversation in the ranks as we plodded along; the prevailing spirit was resolute and grim.

Inside the hall we listened to a robust, stocky man named Severt Young Bear describe what it was like to be besieged at Wounded Knee in the winter of 1973. He spoke of night sorties, fire fights, parachute drops, the extraordinary bravery of ordinary men and women who risked their lives infiltrating federal lines to sneak supplies in to the defenders. On patrol one night a fire fight erupted. Tracers blazed through the air. A bullet struck Young Bear in the leg. His boot filled with blood, making an unpleasant sound when he tried to walk, like a child stomping its foot in a rain puddle. He hobbled awhile, then crawled; incapacitated by the wound, he was finally captured by federal marshals. Though Young Bear's personal involvement was over, the siege continued for several weeks.

Reluctantly, amidst a flurry of groans, we abandoned the warmth of the recreation hall. Buttoning ourselves back up, falling into line, we trekked along a frozen ribbon of asphalt toward Porcupine Butte. A mile south of the village, I saw the only bird I was to see during the entire Big Foot Memorial Ride. A frowzy speck of a thing, dusky and black, it sailed across the road from left to right as if catapulted from a slingshot, disappearing into a copse of iron-stiff trees. "A bird," I gasped to Sherry Mattola and Dana Garber. Sherry didn't hear, or pretended not to. She was plodding like a sleepwalker, her feet encased in lead. "Impossible," growled Dana. "They're all perched on the masts of sailboats cruising the Caribbean."

Sighting Porcupine Butte through the frost-rimmed slit between the bill of my cap and the top of my scarf (masking my nose and mouth), I understood how it got its name. The trees marching up the slope to the bristly crown clearly resembled the quill-studded back of a porcupine. It must have been a vision-questing site, though with the radio station and tower located there now, perhaps it was no longer. It was at this spot, nearly ten years before, where I had picked up Rudy Pretty Hip. I remembered how emotional he'd become in the back seat of the car, breaking down in a fit of sobbing, pressing his face against a filthy rag. How utterly destitute his cries seemed; how powerless my wife and I were to do anything about it. I had looked for Rudy this week; I had made inquiries, but nobody seemed to know where he was, or if they did, they weren't telling.

Before committing ourselves to the final leg of the march into Wounded Knee, Dennis and June-San were to give an interview over KILI radio. We turned off the paved road and made our way as best we could up a rutted, icy path to the broadcast facility, a flimsy-looking structure huddled beneath the tower, under the brow of the tree-crowned summit of Porcupine Butte. The path, with scabby patches of loose gravel poking through crusty layers of snow, swung in a loop across an exposed ridgeline. Within a tantalizing few yards of the door a ferocious wind nearly took our heads off. There was a mad scramble for the door; a few moments later, standing in dazed relief inside the overheated waiting room, we listened to the wind pummel the puny walls. The cold was indescribable; we stood half-paralyzed, spectacles glazed, noses churning, cheeks barked by a whitish discoloration indicating the onset of frostbite. A KILI employee emerged from a studio to announce in a mannerly voice that the temperature outside the groaning walls was fifty below. (The wind-chill index registered ninety below.) Dennis and June-San disappeared into a studio. The rest of us stood around like swaddled mannequins, sipping coffee and chewing stale donuts. It felt a little stupid, suspending the last jag of our walk for a media interview, but it was early afternoon, we were only four miles from our destination, and it wouldn't get dark for several hours. The same employee who announced the temperature now told us that the riders had gotten off to a late start and were at least an hour behind us.

Thirty minutes later Dennis and June-San emerged from the studio. In anticipation of the network cameras sure to be waiting at the foot of the Wounded Knee grave site, Dennis had traded in his sheep's-wool cap for a stunning full-length fox fur. The fox's pointed face perched squarely atop his broad skull, the sharp nose poking over his forehead like the bowsprit of a ship, while the pelt and luxurious tail dangled down his back. "Ohhh, Dennis," cooed a young Indian guy, "you look so *baaaad* . . ." By contrast, the undemonstrative June-San remained cloaked in the same clothes she had worn all week—drab coat, knitted cap, muffling scarf. In another life, she might have been a housewife on her way to the grocery store.

The walk back down the icy path to the asphalt road I will remember as the coldest moment of my entire life. The wind was punishing; sheets of granulated snow swirled around my legs; it felt as if the wind was hammering a steel spike between my eyes. A few feet from the road, Sherry Mattola suddenly faltered. "I can't do it," she groaned. "It's too cold. My strength is gone."

Dana came up on one side, I came up on the other. We huddled close, trying with the bulk of our padded bodies to shield her from the wind. Dana staggered and nearly lost her balance; snatching the sleeve of Sherry's coat, she pulled herself close. "You've got to keep going!" she shouted in Sherry's face. "We're too damn close to quit now! We've come all this way together! We're almost there! You can't give up now! You can't!"

Linking our arms around Sherry's waist, we lurched to the road and took off after the walkers. A few minutes later, under the protective lee of a hill, the wind abated and we caught our breath. Sherry's cheeks were the color of chalk; her lips were blue with discomfort. I offered to tie my scarf to the belt of her coat like a tether, but she shook her head. Somewhere along the way she had picked up a long barkless stick. Clamping both hands around the top, she made a paddling motion and fell into an awkward rhythm that propelled her along the road.

A tribal police car, its roof light throwing a blue flash through the frigid air, led the walkers on the final leg. The time was approximately two o'clock, Friday afternoon, December 28, 1990. A few cars passed, going both ways, slowing to a respectful crawl. Despite the terrific cold, the passengers cranked down the windows and stared silently at the walkers. The passengers were mostly elders, men and women, crowded inside the vehicles, their heads wrapped with shawls or protected by fur caps. They were mostly full bloods, with jowly faces and black, unblinking eyes. At first I couldn't fathom the expressions on their stolid faces. It was strangely unsettling to view those weathered faces framed in the windows of a Ford truck or a Japanese import. And then it came clear why they were here and what they were trying to say. I don't think I misread this; the message came to me in a telepathic flash. One or two lifted their gloved hands in a shy salute, but mostly they just watched us tramp by with a solemn, heartfelt expression. *Wopila.* Thank you. Thank you for braving the terrible cold to honor this moment with us.

A few minutes later, hopping out of a car and sprinting to catch up with us, came Derek Adams. His face was flushed with enthusiasm. "We had to clean up at the school, and I didn't think I'd make it over here in time." He was bundled in a Royal Navy peacoat, with a wool cap pulled down under his ears. "The walk today has generated interest all over the reservation. People at the school have been talking nonstop. They've followed your progress on the radio all day. It's a great moment, an absolutely great moment."

Around three o'clock, footsore and weary, our numbers augmented by new arrivals, we crested the top of the last hill overlooking the shallow basin of Wounded Knee Creek. We were still a good two miles from the grave site. The wind gusted and ebbed. Gauzy skeins of snow swirled across the road, obscuring the horizon. During the lulls we could see all the way into the valley to the smudge of the grave site and the white speck of the Sacred Heart Catholic Church. (The old church had been destroyed by fire in the 1973 uprising.) A strange mix of clouds—some thick, some thin, propelled by the savage wind—swept across the sky. Behind this flowing scrim, with the dullness of a weathered coin, the sun appeared and disappeared, a pallid circle, bloodless and distinct.

What I saw was predictable, a geometrically measurable orb, the perception of an enlightenment mind. What some of those Indians were seeing was entirely different: two glowing orbs, three at times, pulsating and bright, not the icy refractions of a sundog, but something symbolic and evocative, a luminous circle indicative of the sacred hoop; faces shinning from the folds of the passing clouds, heroic faces, familiar faces; and the figures of ancestral riders, cloaked in furs, bedecked with feathers, mounted on sturdy ponies.

Then occurred something, the memory of which I will carry to my dying day. The road looped down a series of tilting slopes to the bottom of the valley. We were maybe a third of the way along when someone shouted, "Riders! The riders!" We looked back up the road to the crest of the watershed dividing Wounded Knee Creek from Porcupine Creek. There, silhouetted against the cloud-tossed sky, as if cut from stiff paper, appeared the advance guard of Big Foot riders. What had been a bare hill, slick with snow, suddenly swarmed with masses of mounted people. Along the road and through the bordering fields they came, bouncing in their hard saddles. Scores of riders, bunched together, strung out in lines, parading in ranks—more people on horseback than I had ever seen in my life. Out front, clad in a flowing red capote, astride a high-stepping black stallion, was Ron McNeill. Poised on the back of the towering horse, he looked imposing; his black hat and eagle feather seemed to touch the sky. To make room for the riders, we crowded to the left side of the road. As McNeill jogged by, we raised our right hands in salute. Like a stone skipping across a pond, he touched the tips of the wavering length of extended fingers and cantered on down the hill.

The other leaders—Arvol Looking House, Birgil Kills Straight, Jim Garrett, a collection of stern-faced elders—swept by soon after on their snorting mounts. Birgil and the others were caparisoned in full ceremonial bonnets tufted with stiff feathers that trailed in long queues down their backs and over the frosty haunches of their horses. Among them was Alex White Plume, wrapped in a buffalo coat and cap, his ruddy face quivering with emotion. Trotting his mount to the midpoint of our line, he rose in the stirrups. Shaking the lance clutched in his right hand, he roared out, "Walkers! You walkers! *Heyupa! Heyupa! Heyupa! Heyupa!*"

The effect was galvanic. An electric shock rippled the length of my body. My right hand, balled in a fist, shot straight up, and I added my own ecstatic shout to the clamor that rolled up and down the line.

The main body of riders enveloped us like a wave. On all sides they appeared, jostling, shivering figures clad in every form of winter dress, ragged and fantastic. Walkers reached up, riders reached down, touching fingers, exchanging grasps, shouting greetings. The horses flooded past, their flanks and bellies mantled with thick crusts of frozen sweat. In a sweeping tide, down from the top of the hill, saddles creaking, hooves plopping, they came in a steady flood, men, women, children, shaking staffs and lances, singing at the tops of their lungs. The surge was unstoppable; finally united after five days, riders and walkers poured off that hill with irresistible force. The moment was incandescent. I saw Fred Brown Bull, who waved exultantly, and, behind him, little Roy, who called, "Beezy! Hey, Beezy!" On and on they came, lapping us on both sides, smelling of hard yellow sweat and fresh horse dung; the two groups mingled triumphantly for a few delicious moments. Gradually the riders thinned out; in their wake came a trickle of stragglers who kicked at their mounts to catch up. Riding drag as he had all week, clad in a soiled white duster, grim-faced and preoccupied, a silk scarf binding his skull, came Percy White Plume. Somebody called out his name, but he didn't glance our direction.

It took another hour to reach the grave site. New people joined us for the homestretch. Veterans in wheelchairs were lifted out of vans and wheeled into line. I looked for Phoebe Running Hawk, but the awful cold evidently had kept her away. On down the final slope and onto the level stretch west of the creek we marched in a close-knit column. People stood at the side of the road taking pictures; the anticipated media blitz had failed to materialize. A couple of people with video cameras hung on our flanks, but no network stuff, though maybe they had already filmed the riders and packed up and disappeared. Alone, largely unnoticed, amidst a confusion of people wandering across the road and vehicles turning around, we finished our walk into Wounded Knee. Above the clump of stiff boots against the pavement came the steady tap of the drum, the steady drone of chanting.

By the time we pulled in, the riders had already formed their circle, completed their prayers, and were in the process of disbanding, pulling the saddles off their weary mounts, rubbing them with towels, loading them into trailers. Dennis and June-San led the walkers off the road, between a scattering of parked trailers and pickups, to an open space at the foot of the grave-site knoll where we grouped ourselves into a final circle. George White Thunder, who had carried the lance the entire distance since our descent from Porcupine Butte, finally turned it over to Dennis. Two boys with bags of tobacco made a circuit of the inside rim of the circle; we each took a pinch in our left hand and held it over our head. An Ojibway medicine man who had joined us at Porcupine Butte was invited by Dennis to make the final prayer. As the words rang out in the man's native tongue, I looked up at the graveyard at the top of the knoll. A harsh wind, skimming across the crown, kicked up plumes of powdery snow. The wrought-iron portal marking the grave site arched across the leaden sky like a croquet wicket. The obelisk containing the names of the Miniconjous who had died on this spot a hundred years ago stuck up from the rectangular plot like a marble thumb.

The Ojibway medicine man completed his prayer. At a signal from Dennis, we released the tobacco between our fingers; the wind caught the flakes and sent them spinning. Something else went out from me, a wordless prayer accompanied by a double memory of my dead mother and grandmother, maternal figures of invincible generosity. Dennis stepped to the center of the circle. The nose of the bright orange fox peered inquisitively over his forehead. "It is finished," he announced. "Our walk is completed. We have honored the memory of our ancestors. I thank the spirits for guiding us safely to our destination. I thank the cold weather for making us strong. *Mitakuye oyasin*—we are all related."

He stepped back, bowed his head, and it was over. The circle hung together for a few more moments, then broke apart. People stood off by themselves, exhausted and spent; others groped together in clumsy embraces. Shivers rippled through Sherry Mattola's shoulders as I gave her a hug. Her eyes were damp, her lips fixed in a smile of relief. Derek Adams' black beard was stiff with frost; he blinked quickly, looked away, then blinked again. "We have to take this home with us, wherever we live, and give it back to everyone we know." His soft English voice was fiercely pitched. He clutched the lapels of my parka and pressed his cold cheek against mine. "That's how we make a difference in the world, bit by bit, piece by piece. We can do it, you know. We can change it all for the better."

I shook Dennis's hand and thanked him for his leadership. One by one, accompanied by formal bows, I exchanged salutations with the Japanese. And so it went—Pagan, Dana, Bob Keyes, Bo de Sitter, all the friends I had made in the past week. An uneasy feeling crept through my stomach. It was over. The circle, the chanting, the drum taps, the endless walking—I had no idea what I was going to do next. I felt happy, at peace, fulfilled; at the same time I felt inexpressibly sad.

In the shift of people saying their farewells, an opening suddenly appeared. Standing by himself at the edge of the circle was George White Thunder. I moved toward him, hugged him affectionately, then stepped back. He seemed absorbed in an emotion beyond the propriety of the moment for me to personally share. He was Lakota, I was white; for all the solidarity we had just experienced, there were differences that no amount of sympathy or imagination could overcome.

The cold bore down; the wind swirled anew. Snow danced in vigorous spurts on top of the graveyard. It was finished, and my heart seemed to flake into a thousand pieces, each piece weighted with the burden of an inconsolable sorrow. George stood by himself, solitary and grieving. He raised his mittened fingers to his face. Making a steady fanning motion with the backs of both hands, he wiped the tears that fell from his mournful brown eyes.

10

Anyone, Indian or otherwise, that was not among the group in the center who were encircled by the soldiers, cannot tell the actual truth of what really happened. It is true that the soldiers have to make reports of their actions, but their reports must be in their favor and recorded as such; they are required to carry on warfare under certain laws and regulations and they know that they must not go beyond these laws and regulations and have to give an account of their actions, therefore their reports must show that they were right and could not be blamed in no way, so they make reports without opposition in their favor, Indians and others who have heard the reports of the soldiers as above stated retold it in the same manner as reported by the soldiers.

While with the survivors it is entirely different, they are not compelled to make a report, nor to follow any legal instruction so they have not on record anywhere an account of what really happened, no one defended them, but were blamed for all that occurred. We have not said anything for the reason that what we might say would not be regarded as the truth, the United States Government never did investigate this affair to find out the real truth and have so recorded it to this day.

—*Joseph Black Hair, quoted in* The Wounded Knee Massacre *by James H. McGregor (1940)*

Colonel Forsyth's ringing plea for his men to cease fire did not take effect as quickly as he might have hoped. The majority of Indians within the vicinity of the campsite were either dead or dying, but those who managed to escape the inferno, first inside the council ring, then down in the ravine, were still being pursued. On foot or by horse, with single-minded relentlessness, the troopers tracked the survivors across the plains. They followed them into ditches; they flushed them from brush patches; they forced them out from behind stunted trees—women and children mainly, a few elders. The majority of fighting men had already been annihilated in the council circle or inside the ravine. Some of the survivors were called upon to surrender before being fired upon; half-frozen, frantic with terror, dazed with shock, they were shot down like dogs. The sound of gunfire persisted until early afternoon. Bodies were found as far as three miles from the campsite.

The butchery was appalling. The stories come down not from historical sources which are terse and limited in detail but through Lakota oral traditions, which are profuse and descriptive. The contrast is striking enough to raise the suspicion that either someone is exaggerating or someone else is withholding the truth. Recounted on the printed page, the catalogue of verifiable facts seems curiously incomplete. The exact tally of Miniconjou dead has never been accurately determined. Lakota estimates run as high as three hundred or more. Official military statistics indicate maybe half that number. One hundred and forty-six bodies (eighty-four men and boys, forty-four women, eighteen children) were retrieved from within a two-hundred-yard area; this number, however, failed to include those who were killed a mile or two away while trying to flee, or those whose bodies were carried off by friends and relatives, or those who died of wounds in the Pine Ridge hospital. (Fifty-one wounded were admitted for treatment, seven of whom died, bringing the official army total to one hundred and fifty-three.)

The stories that come down through Lakota oral traditions are horrific. Told around campfires, told around pot-bellied stoves, told over kitchen tables, the stories have been passed from generation to generation. Every Lakota family on a South Dakota reservation has stories about what happened to their ancestors that day—stories about skulls being bashed in with rifle butts, stories about stomachs being ripped open with sabers, stories about victims being riddled by bullets long after they were dead. Sidney Bird, who grew up near Wounded Knee Creek in the 1930s listening to the old men of the community tell their versions of the event, insists that the hearts of the white men who executed the deed were full of evil. "What else would compel them to behave so outrageously?" he asks.

Two examples among many will suffice. A woman, fleeing the carnage, tried to protect two children (evidently not her own). A trooper on horseback took off after her. Bringing her to bay, he methodically shot the two children with his rifle, knocking them out of the woman's arms. Reloading, the trooper then shot the woman, who toppled over backwards. Badly wounded, she pretended to be dead. The trooper dismounted and stepped to where she lay; with the point of his saber, he lifted the hem of her skirt. Satisfied with whatever he was seeking, he got back on his horse and rode off.

Another is told by Leonard Little Finger, who heard it from his grandfather. After the shooting in the ravine ceased, soldiers went around kicking the victims. If they moved, the soldiers shot them again. A woman with a baby in her arms sat on the ground, rocking back and forth. A soldier grabbed the baby out of her arms and threw it on the ground and fired two shots. The woman leaped to her feet and ran for the baby; with the barrel of the pistol, the soldier hit her on the back of the head and knocked her down. Then he pressed his boot against her throat. Then he fired the pistol four times into her body.

There were even a few white witnesses who were surprised by the ferocity of the killing. An unnamed trooper quoted by Bruce Nelson in *Land of the Dacotahs* (1946) said that after the firing ceased "the women lay thick. One girl about eighteen was supporting herself on her hand, the blood spurting from her mouth as from a pump. Near her lay two others, and all around, like patches of snow, were dead squaws, each in a pool of blood. Colonel Forsyth looked very white as he gave orders to see if any of the women who lay thick around were alive. From the blanket of one we took a boy five years old and a baby about as many months—both unhurt, but the mother was dead. She must have been shot with a revolver held not five feet away, as her hair was burned and the skin blackened with powder."

In Pine Ridge that morning, eighteen miles to the west, the rumble of gunfire could clearly be heard. Alarmed by the sound, a number of warriors snatched up their weapons and galloped east over the prairie. One of them was Black Elk, later to achieve fame for his autobiography. He saddled his buckskin horse and donned a shirt decorated with a spotted eagle on the back, a daybreak star on the left shoulder, and two rainbows across the chest—representations of one of his most powerful visions. He painted his face red and tied a single feather in his hair. Riding alone, he arrived in time to witness the Hotchkiss guns at the top of the knoll shatter the last pockets of protection inside the ravine. Along with a handful of warriors, he managed to rescue a few Miniconjous. He had no gun. Holding a sacred bow in front of him, he charged the soldiers; their bullets zinged harmlessly past his ears. At one point he discovered a little girl lying alone in a remote part of the ravine; wrapping her in a shawl, he tucked her in a safe place. The ravine was littered with the bodies of women and children and infants. The taste of revenge filled his mouth like sour blood. Again and again, Black Elk and the others charged the soldiers, but there were too many of them and their firepower was too strong. Only after the shooting stopped did the warriors break off their attacks. Retrieving the little girl, cradling her in the crook of his arm, Black Elk rode back toward Pine Ridge.

The carnage along Wounded Knee Creek was appalling. The tents and tipis of the Miniconjous had been pulverized by cannon shot. Fires still burned; the reek of charred flesh filled the air. Bodies were strewn everywhere: face down, on their backs, torn and spattered with blood, mouths contorted in rigid grimaces, arms and legs twisted in agonizing postures. Bodies were heaped in stacks, tangled in blankets and loose clothing. Mothers clutched dead children; old people reached out with empty fingers; warriors gripped rifles and bows. It was as if a gigantic threshing machine had moved inexorably through the council ring and campsite and down into the ravine, chewing, shredding, puncturing; the terrible firepower put forth by the soldiers and the Hotchkiss guns had decimated the Miniconjous with rivening force.

As soon as the shooting stopped, the wounded were tended to. First aid was suddenly being administered everywhere; people who just a scant few minutes before had been mercilessly gunned down were swabbed and bandaged and loaded into ambulances and freight wagons for the trip to Pine Ridge. Despite having been stabbed in the lungs, Father Francis Craft, S.J., moved persistently among the casualties, administering last rites till his strength gave out and he crumpled to the ground. Seventh Cavalry victims ran high—thirty soldiers were killed outright or eventually succumbed to their wounds. The majority were slain by their own men, in a deadly crossfire that whipped back and forth across the council ring.

Word of the debacle made its way to Pine Ridge with mystifying speed. (A military courier and an Indian runner, who left the site at approximately the same time, arrived in Pine Ridge at about the same time.) Camped close to the agency, as a gesture of trust and good will, were some four thousand Brules and Oglalas. Among them was the Two Strike faction, die-hard ghost dancers, followers of Short Bull and Kicking Bear, who, pressed by the weather and lack of food, had trickled in the week before. News of the violence threw the camp in an uproar. With the bulk of his troops at Wounded Knee Creek, General John Brooke had few resources to call upon to protect his headquarters from a retaliatory attack. A platoon of Oglala tribal police drew themselves up in a ring around the headquarters building. Shouts, cries, roars of anger rang through the air; shots were fired, but the police and the sprinkling of soldiers held their positions. General Brooke wisely ordered his men not to fire back, thus avoiding what undoubtedly would have been a bloody shootout. Instead, the angry Indians dismantled their tipis and disappeared over the hills to the north.

Around 9:30 that evening, the first wagons escorted by cavalry clattered into Pine Ridge. The pews inside the Holy Cross Episcopal Church were removed, and the Miniconjou wounded were carried inside and placed on quilts and blankets on the straw-padded floor. (Army wounded were transferred to hospital tents.) Dr. Charles Eastman, a full-blood Santee Sioux, aided by his wife-to-be, Elaine Goodale, assisted by a few nurses and orderlies, did what he could to make the survivors comfortable. "Many were frightfully torn by pieces of shells, and the suffering was terrible," Dr. Eastman later wrote in his memoirs. When army surgeons tried to help, the Indians recoiled in terror at being attended to by men in uniform. Lacking proper medicines and surgical facilities, many wounded perished during the night. Others, both adults and children, survived against daunting odds. Wounded fourteen times, a woman named Blue Whirlwind eventually recovered. Several children whose parents had been killed also recovered and were later adopted by white families. (The most famous of these was a little girl named Lost Bird. Taken in by the family of the commander of the Nebraska National Guard, she was destined for a lonely death in California in the 1930s; her remains were finally returned to the common graveyard atop the knoll in 1991.)

Tortured with pain, moaning in agony, the patients during that long night sank into a stupor of terrible suffering. Dr. Eastman worked patiently over each, applying what medicines he had, speaking soothingly in Lakota. The Christmas decorations festooning the church walls provided a mocking commentary to his diligent labors. Outside the church, Brule and Oglala elders gathered. The women cut their hair and beat their breasts with their fists; the men filled the air with the piteous cry of their death songs.

During the night the weather turned foul. A cutting wind blew from the northwest (as it would again, one hundred years later), bringing with it a heavy snowfall. The bodies of the slain Miniconjous, left lying on the field, were contorted into grotesque positions. The official burial crew, contracted by the army, delayed by bad weather and a disagreement over the price per corpse, did not arrive on the scene until January 3, 1891. They were accompanied by a military escort. The foul weather had passed, and, working without coats, the crew hacked a rectangular trench along an east-west alignment across the crown of the knoll where the Hotchkiss guns had done their deadly work. While the crew picked at the frozen ground, two photographers, George Trager and Clarence Moreledge, took pictures of the devastated campsite and the bodies of the fallen Miniconjous. Partially covered with snow, his head bound in a scarf, dressed in bulky *wasicu* clothing, Big Foot lay propped up in a semireclining posture. His eyes were sealed, his mouth creased in a rigid line, his fingers curled like stiff petals.

Wagons heaped with cadavers rumbled to the top of the knoll; souvenir hunters among the soldiers and civilians had already stripped many of the bodies. Ghost shirts were a prized item, as well as moccasins, blankets, parfleches, buffalo horns, and weapons such as war clubs and bows and arrows. So brisk was the sale of souvenirs that a correspondent for the *New York Herald* wrote on January 26, "The dealers in trinkets are selling all of the Indian goods they can secure, and at prices that are fabulous . . . Tenderfeet have already purchased . . . at least a carload of ghost shirts that Big Foot was supposed to have had on at the time he was killed."

With little fanfare, the cadavers of men, women, and children were unloaded from the wagons and stacked inside the mass grave like logs in a fire pit. After several layers had been deposited, members of the burial crew pressed the weight of their feet against chests and faces and upflung limbs to make room for more. Soldiers and civilians posed for pictures standing next to the yawning pit. Jokes were exchanged; a festive atmosphere prevailed. It took several hours to bury all the bodies. Dirt was finally shoveled in. In all, 146 bodies were interred. The crew tamped the rounded mound with the flat of their shovels. Soldiers pounded the loose dirt with the butts of their rifles. Then the party packed up and departed, leaving the wind to claw at the crown of the knoll. No Catholic priest or Protestant minister spoke any words. No consideration was given to the possibility of individual graves. That night and for many nights to come, stealthily and in small groups, relatives and friends of the dead crept to the grave site, leaving prayer sticks, tobacco ties, and ceremonial flags.

Within twenty-four hours of the debacle, Colonel Forsyth

was in trouble again. The morning after the massacre, Drexel Mission, located four miles north of Pine Ridge, officiated by a kindly priest named Father Jutz, was attacked by angry warriors. Boots and saddles was sounded; four troops of the Seventh Cavalry, with Colonel Forsyth in the lead, rode to the rescue. (Actually, the mission wasn't under attack; Father Jutz was so highly regarded by the Brule and Oglala that neither he nor his associates were harmed. A schoolhouse nearby was burned to the ground.)

The mission was located in a valley, enveloped by steep hills. Failing to adequately protect his flanks, Forsyth led his men, four hundred strong, into a trap. From the tops of the hills, from concealed positions near the mission, about fifty warriors poured forth a concentrated fire. (Black Elk was among them, armed this time, eager for vengeance.) Five men were wounded, one private was killed. Lieutenant James D. Mann, who had issued the warning of danger to K Troop the day before, received wounds that would prove fatal. Pinned down, unable to target the elusive enemy, the troopers lost heart. A courier was sent galloping back to Pine Ridge. To the rescue, guidons flapping, came the Ninth Cavalry, led by Major Guy Henry, a first-rate officer. The Ninth was composed of "buffalo soldiers," battle-tested black troopers whose courage and toughness had earned them the respect of both Indians and white soldiers. The morning they rode to Forsyth's rescue, the black troopers were numb with fatigue. Word of the shooting at Wounded Knee had reached them the previous afternoon when they were on patrol in the Badlands; they had marched eighty miles through a blinding snowstorm, reaching Pine Ridge at dawn. Unrolling their blankets, they barely had time to stretch out their saddle-weary bodies when they were called upon to mount up again and push their limping horses at a steady trot to Drexel Mission. Major Henry sent a pair of flanking columns up the slopes behind a barrage of Hotchkiss shells, which quickly cleared the hills of hostiles. A swift charge scattered the last pockets in the valley. So overjoyed were many of the white soldiers of the Seventh Cavalry, they embraced their black liberators. Colonel Forsyth's comments to

Major Henry upon being saved from this humiliating situation were not recorded.

By telegraph the morning of December 30, a sanitized version of the events of the previous day reached U.S. Army headquarters in Washington, D.C. Commander in Chief John M. Schofield wired his congratulations back to Pine Ridge, citing the successful disarmament of Big Foot's followers with a minimum of bloodshed. The next day, accounts of a significantly different story began to crop up in the Eastern press. Initially, only two military fatalities were reported; as the list increased and the magnitude of the Miniconjou casualties became apparent, the high brass in the nation's capital became concerned.

Closer to the scene, first at his headquarters in Rapid City, then on a train chugging to Chadron, Nebraska, General Nelson A. Miles, commander of the Department of the Missouri, began to collect some disturbing evidence. Upon arriving in Pine Ridge on December 31, Miles telegraphed General Schofield that his congratulations to the Seventh Cavalry may have been premature. Miles waited a few days to accumulate more evidence. On January 2, 1891, he wired Schofield that, contrary to first reports, "the action of the Colonel commanding will . . . undoubtedly be the subject of investigation." By the end of the second day of the new year, both General Schofield and President Benjamin Harrison were in possession of a much fuller account of the bloodshed. Shocked by the magnitude of the violence, Eastern humanitarian groups began bombarding the White House with complaints. Schofield reported that the president was "very unhappy." After consulting with Harrison, Schofield wired Miles the president's regrets that the disarming had not gone smoothly and directed that "an inquiry be made as to the killing of women and children on Wounded Knee Creek."

This was the signal Miles was waiting for. On January 4, "by direction of the President," he relieved Forsyth of command and appointed a board of inquiry. In so doing, however, he overstepped his own authority. General Schofield had ordered him to initiate an inquiry; he had not granted him the right to take specific action and relieve Forsyth of command. The fuzziness of the wording of the directive enabled Miles, in his own mind at least, to carry out what he thought was best for everyone involved. The board of inquiry began taking testimonies from officers and enlisted men. Aware of the political nature of the inquiry, the board proceeded carefully. On January 18, a conclusion was delivered. The board censured Forsyth for the placement of his troops, but exonerated him of all wrong-doing in regard to the loss of Miniconjou lives. Casualties among women and children, the board declared (in language as fuzzy as that delivered by President Harrison or General Schofield), "could be ascribed only to the fault of the Indians themselves and the force of unavoidable and unfortunate circumstances."

Miles was not ready to give up. He ordered another investigation, this one aimed at indicting Forsyth for mishandling the Drexel Mission engagement. These charges were subsequently dismissed by General Schofield and Secretary of War Redfield Proctor. It is difficult to say for certain why Miles's charges failed to stick. On the surface his case seemed solid. Forsyth had clearly proven himself incompetent, both at handling Indians in touchy situations and in handling the conduct of his own troops in battle. Personal animosity toward Miles at the highest levels was probably a factor; another was the political sensitivity of the matter among some of President Harrison's Republican backers. Wounded Knee had the makings of a first-rate scandal, with the potential for soiling reputations and careers. A bitter court-martial, with Miles center stage, advancing his own ambitions, would attract more press. More press would lead to more investigations. More investigations would reveal more facts about an event which, botched in execution and disastrous in consequences, was best concealed from prying eyes behind a veil of half-truths. Miles himself recognized the explosive nature of the issue; in 1897, when he published a memoir of his Indian-fighting exploits as a means of making his name better known to the American public, he made no mention of Wounded Knee. A hint of how anxious officials were to conceal the real truth can be gleaned from the text of General Schofield's final decision on the matter. "The interests of the military service," he stated, "do not demand any further proceedings in this case." To Miles's dismay, Colonel Forsyth was reinstated as commander of the Seventh Cavalry.

The achievement of Standing Soldier, an Oglala scout for the U.S. Army, underscores the ineptness of Forsyth's handling of the affair. Sent out to apprehend seventy-three Hunkpapa warriors and their families who had fled Sitting Bull's encampment on the Grand River in the wake of the old chief's death, Standing Soldier brought the entire contingent to Pine Ridge on the evening of December 30, without losing a member of his fifteen-man squad and without harming any of the Hunkpapas. He achieved this remarkable feat through a combination of tact and deceit. When he first encountered the Hunkpapas on December 27, he told them they could keep their weapons; he then ordered his own men to share their rations and tobacco. The next day, when the Hunkpapas complained of hunger, Standing Soldier had his men kill and butcher several cattle from an abandoned ranch. Intersecting Big Foot's trail on the morning of the twenty-eighth, Standing Soldier sent couriers to tell the chief to proceed no further, though by the time the couriers came within sight of the Miniconjous, they were already in the escort of Major Whitside. On the morning of the twenty-ninth, with gunfire booming to the south and the Hunkpapas acting fidgety and upset, Standing Soldier, suspecting the worst, reassured them that all that was happening was a series of friendly salutes. That night a courier from Pine Ridge arrived in his camp with an order from Standing Soldier's superior, Lieutenant Charles W. Taylor, to disarm the Hunkpapas and break up their weapons. Standing Soldier ignored the order, and sent the courier back with a message stating that he would bring in the Hunkpapas on his own and if Lieutenant Taylor wished to disarm them, he could do so himself. The following evening, before entering Pine Ridge, Standing Soldier made a prayer to the Christian God, saying that all Indians must learn to live in peace with the white man. He reminded the Hunkpapas that he and his scouts had risked their lives to bring them safely to Pine Ridge, then he asked the warriors to turn over their weapons to their women. With scouts covering the flanks, Standing Soldier prodded the Hunkpapas all the way to the door of General Brooke's headquarters. When the general heard from the Hunkpapas' own mouths that they were willing to surrender their weapons, he thanked them politely and ordered a full complement of rations for them to feed on.

Bureaucratic systems breed their own protective mechanisms. Not only was Colonel Forsyth reinstated, but by 1894 he was promoted to brigadier general. Three years later he attained the rank of major general. By 1895, Miles himself, despite opposition, rose to the top of the heap, replacing General Schofield as commander in chief. The ironies don't stop there. Colonel Edwin Sumner, whom Miles had chastised for allowing Big Foot's band to slip away from the Cheyenne River, was elevated to the leadership of the Seventh Cavalry. But the crowning irony, an event that galled General Miles and that sticks like a bone in the throat of every Lakota to this day, was the awarding of eighteen Medals of Honor, the nation's highest combat decoration, to three officers and fifteen enlisted men for "uncommon valor" at the "battle" of Wounded Knee Creek.

For the remainder of his life, Miles maintained that Forsyth had blundered and that the Miniconjous deserved some form of compensation for their suffering. On March 13, 1917, at the age of seventy-seven, Lieutenant General Nelson A. Miles, U.S. Army (retired), addressed the Commissioner of Indian Affairs in the following words:

> In my opinion, the least the government can do is to make a suitable recompense to the survivors for the great injustice which was done to them and the serious loss of their relatives and property. The action of the commanding officer, in my judgment at the time, and I so reported, was most reprehensible. The disposition of the troops was such that in firing upon the warriors, they fired directly toward their own lines and also into the camp of the women and children, and I have regarded the whole affair as most unjustifiable and worthy of the severest condemnation.

It is ironic to find General Miles, the decorated Indian fighter, playing the role of protector in this matter. But nothing about Wounded Knee is easy to understand. The complexities and complications will never be fully elucidated. Considering the bloody pageant that unfolded throughout the hemisphere following Columbus's first landfall, it seems only appropriate that the last major confrontation between natives and *wasicu* should end in disaster. But the perception of disaster by the public was precisely what the Harrison administration wanted to avoid. Four hundred years after Columbus, with most of the Indians in the hemisphere either dead or confined to reservations, with humanitarian groups in favor of transforming those who remained from nomadic infidels to yeoman Christians, public relations had become a critical component of domestic policy. By 1890 image was of paramount importance in dealing with native people. General Miles knew this. President Harrison knew this. You couldn't kill Indians indiscriminately as Custer had along the Washita River in 1868 or John M. Chivington had along Sand Creek in 1864. By 1890 the preferred instrument of conquest was assimilation—forbidding them to speak their language or practice their religion, dressing them in *wasicu* clothing, forcing them to live in box-like houses. Only when these adjustments had been accomplished could the final indignity be added: rewriting their struggle to survive the bloody abattoir at Wounded Knee so that its particulars could be seamlessly woven into the fabric of a mythical tapestry depicting the glorious conquest of an empty continent by a superior race.

As a coda to all this—in the interest of retaining the long perspective—it's helpful to remember that, to this day, neither the federal government nor the U.S. Army has ever issued an apology for their actions, nor has any recompense been offered to the families of either the victims or the survivors of the massacre.

Installed at his new headquarters in Pine Ridge, Nelson Miles was busy with more than just the prosecution of Colonel Forsyth for his putative misdeeds. Panicked by the bloody events at Wounded Knee, thousands of Indians had folded their tents and fled the encampment at Pine Ridge; their destination was the desolate terrain of the Badlands, specifically the isolated bastion of Stronghold Table. Among their ranks were the major

Ghost Dance leaders—Short Bull, Kicking Bear, and Two Strike. Among them also were several Oglala "progressives"—Little Wound, Big Road, and No Water. Red Cloud was also along, albeit not of his own volition; in the wake of the furor over Wounded Knee, he claimed to have been kidnapped and forced to flee with the others.

Red Cloud remained precariously neutral during the Ghost Dance troubles. Nearly seventy years old, growing feeble, cataracts clouding his eyes, the old chief knew that resistance was futile. He had not always felt that way; in his prime he had fought fiercely against the white invaders. Along the Bozeman Trail in 1866, he had helped devise the decoy strategy that tempted Captain William Fetterman to lead eighty men to their deaths. Several trips back east, one in particular to New York City in 1870 where he addressed an enthusiastic crowd at Cooper Union, taught the canny Oglala that the *wasicu* were too numerous and too strong. He realized then that it was best that the Lakota not antagonize them unnecessarily, in order to secure the best possible deal for themselves in the future. When the Ghost Dance turmoil erupted, Red Cloud declared his neutrality and refused to be swayed by either the dancers or the progressives. A few observers tried to blame him for the deviltry, but the charges wouldn't stick. A firebrand in his youth, a tough negotiator in his middle years, by his dotage Red Cloud had settled into a stoical acceptance of the white man's ways.

All those Indians roaming the countryside posed a vexing problem for Miles. His primary concern was the possibility of renewed violence. On the afternoon of New Year's Day, a Sixth Cavalry wagon train bumping along the White River valley was attacked by a band of warriors. A sharp fight ensued; the warriors were finally driven off after losing six men. With four thousand soldiers at his disposal, Miles began to tighten the screws. On all sides, from the White River in the north to the Nebraska border in the south, from Wounded Knee Creek in the east to Pine Ridge in the west, the net of infantry and cavalry began to close upon the beleaguered Lakota. Drawing upon the tactics that had garnered him success in the past—gentle persuasion laced with threats of ruthless force—Miles sought to convince the Lakota of the futility of further resistance.

Despite sporadic outbreaks, including the random killings of a white cook and a cavalry officer, the violence gradually subsided. Within the ranks of the Lakota a rift occurred between the Oglalas, who wanted to return to the safety of Pine Ridge, and the Brules, who remained openly defiant. The night of January 8, Red Cloud and a party of cohorts crept out of their own camp and slipped away south toward Pine Ridge. Red Cloud's defection was demoralizing to the Oglalas who remained. The return to the reservation of the influential chief Young-Man-Afraid-of-His-Horses from a two-month trip to Montana provided a shot of confidence to the spirits of the progressives who wanted to bring their people in. The resolve of the Brule hard-liners began to crumble. Each day brought more defections. Wary of precipitating another Wounded Knee, Miles cautioned his commanders not to press too close. The last remnants of Brule resistance finally dissipated, and on January 15, 1891, an impressive assembly of several thousand Lakota—mounted and pulling travois, with scouts in the lead and *akicita* hovering at the flanks and bringing up the rear—marched into Pine Ridge. "It was a spectacle worth beholding," an officer noted—the last concentrated display of Indian armed strength on the North American continent. The chiefs announced that they would collect their warriors' weapons; when they failed to gather them all, Miles did not insist that they be accountable for the rest. Though there was no formal act of surrender, a symbolic denouement of sorts took place when the Brule chief Kicking Bear, an apostle of the old ways, a disciple of Wovoka—with a flash of defiance in his eyes—placed his rifle at the feet of General Miles. The Ghost Dance troubles were over.

A week later, the army staged its own demonstration of power. Criers went through the Brule and Oglala camps the night before, announcing that a review was to take place the next day. With matters returning to normal on the northern plains, units were being reassigned to other parts of the country. As General Miles sat on a coal-black horse on a hillside overlooking a long valley, the entire contingent of troops, some thirty-five hundred men, passed in review. Indians stood at the tops of both slopes, facing each other across the valley; there were hundreds of them, and they were wrapped in blankets, their faces stony and expressionless. (On foot, disarmed, they were spectators this time with no means to resist—hostages in the heart of their own country.) A vicious wind funneled the length of the valley, kicking up clouds of yellow dust. Through the murk, marching in close formation, came the infantry behind their commander, Colonel William R. Shafter. Then came the artillery: heavy howitzers, squads of Gatling guns, the crews of the Hotchkiss batteries. Then came the cavalry, the storied units that had distinguished themselves in countless campaigns during the past quarter century. The wind swirled and danced, generating an unpleasant haze which made it difficult to see. During the entire time the troops passed in review, not a single cheer was heard, not a single huzzah; as they drew abreast of General Miles, orders were delivered in muffled voices, swords were snapped from their scabbards, rifles were raised, and eyes pivoted with synchronized precision toward the figure, draped in a civilian overcoat with no insignia showing, sitting astride a black horse. As the Sixth Cavalry passed, with crusty old Colonel E. H. Carr out front, General Miles swept the wide-brimmed hat from his head. Following Carr, in close lines, their carbines held at salute, came Major Guy Henry's buffalo soldiers, bundled in heavy coats and fur caps. The wind continued to whip and froth. Last to pass was the Seventh Cavalry; in Colonel Forsyth's absence, Major Samuel Whitside led the command. As the front line paraded past Miles, the buglers let out a blast and the regimental band struck up the "Garry Owen," Custer's famous marching song. Overcome with emotion, Miles hung his hat on the pommel of his saddle and let the capricious wind ruffle his iron-gray locks. The troopers flung back their capes, exposing the lemon-colored linings; as each rank drew even with Miles, they presented their carbines in salute. Infected by the sprightly rhythm of the march, the horses high-stepped smartly. And then it was over. The last rank passed with a snap of rifles. General Miles capped the black hat back on his head and prodded his horse on down the slope. The wind twisted and fumed, casting veils of pale dust over the faces of the silent Lakota, who remained looking at one another across the valley for a long time after the soldiers had disappeared.

11

Oh, Sun, forgive me the renegade thought: I love with my whole heart the old ways of the Indian.

—*Thomas H. Leforge,* Memoirs of a White Crow Indian *(1928)*

It was over—the walking, the circling up, the praying, the drum beats, the chanting. I felt spent and deflated like a tire suddenly emptied of cushioning air. It was over, and suddenly the complicated machinery of interacting parts—the cooks, the gofers, the support vehicles, the wranglers, the riders and walkers—would disappear from view. It was over, and the cohesiveness that had brought us together would gradually crumble, and, solitary and detached, we would drift back to our ordinary lives. In a day or two, I would leave the reservation. There would no longer be any place to stay, there would no longer be anything to eat, there would be nothing left to do. It was over, and the closeness we had experienced, the heady tonic of sacralized travel, would be replaced by the mundane business of getting on in life.

But it wasn't over yet. There was still the ceremony at the grave site tomorrow morning, at which the riders would appear for a final time. For now, packed into Bob Keyes's car, stupefied with cold, a bunch of us motored to the high school in Manderson. Inside the gym a crowd had gathered. Before a microphone on a curtained stage, people were stepping forward to speak their thoughts. Young and old, men and women, local celebrities and unknowns, if they had something to say, came forth and delivered. We sat down on the hard wooden bleachers and unzipped our heavy coats and continued the process of thawing out that had begun in Bob's car. Fresh coffee was available; in a little while, from the kitchen off to one side, another feed of buffalo soup would be offered. It wasn't over yet; there were others to hear from, more ceremonies to perform, more events to observe. The speakers droned on. Nobody paid much attention. An Indian congressman from Colorado spoke. The chairman of the Oglala Tribal Council spoke. The same bitter guy who had denounced white people on Christmas Eve around the council fire denounced them again, in almost exactly the same words. (The harshness of his tone seemed out of place in the wake of the good feelings engendered by the final day's ride.) It wasn't over yet. Here in the high school at six this evening a press conference was scheduled. Sound trucks from the major networks were already idling in the parking lot; technicians were lugging in equipment. Tomorrow night a powwow was to be held at the Little Wound School, a major powwow, with dancers and drummers from all the South Dakota reservations.

Between speakers, there was a feather ceremony to acknowledge the youngest of the Big Foot riders, an eight-year-old boy named Joshua Moon Guerro. As Arvol Looking Horse prayed over the feather, the audience grew hushed and attentive. Arvol had shed a few of the layers he had worn this afternoon on the way into Wounded Knee. After blessing the feather, which had been donated by Alex White Plume, Arvol handed it to Rocky Afraid of Hawk, one of the original nineteen riders, who tied it to Josh's hair. To the fury of a hidden drum, a selection of twenty-five riders commenced to circle the boy in a fluid configuration from three different directions, which gave each rider the opportunity to reach out and touch the boy's hair at least three times. Josh remained rooted to the spot, his hands clasped in front of his belt, his face radiant with pride.

The news conference began shortly after six. Bob, Bo, and I squeezed into the overflowing room. A battery of cameras had been set up, and the klieg lights were beaming. The TV people fiddled with their equipment with that self-important air they seem to display wherever they go. A few minutes later the *Sitanka Wokiksuye* leaders, fresh from the ride, filed into the room: Birgil Kills Straight, Arvol Looking Horse, Ron McNeill, Alex White Plume, and Jim Garrett. The impact of the terrible cold congealed like a transparent syrup on their weary faces. Neither Dennis Banks nor Russell Means was present. The politics of the situation were obviously complicated, though there was no way, at the close of the Big Foot Ride, that the organizers were going to share the podium with the American Indian Movement. AIM was too controversial; although its influence in Pine Ridge was negligible, the presence of its two best-known leaders stirred powerful emotions. The purpose of the ride was to bring people together, to bind up the wounds, to bridge the divisiveness between rival factions. Consensus politics was never a strong suit with AIM. Their role in the week's activities had been wisely limited to the meeting Thursday night in the lunchroom of the Little Wound School. Though they could no longer attract a crowd, they could play the role of the spoiler (as Russell Means would do tomorrow morning at the grave site). Whatever media goodies there were to be savored in the aftermath of the successful completion of the Big Foot Ride belonged to the five men who now settled themselves at the long table in front of the array of cameras.

No doubt Banks and Means would have exploited the opportunity for national exposure for all it was worth. Not so the Big Foot organizers. They were low-keyed and informative; they seemed intent upon clarifying the reasons underlying the ride. Their restraint was commendable; the complex emotions many of the participants had experienced coming into Wounded Knee this afternoon could not be telescoped into the abbreviated format of the evening news. Instead of boasting about their accomplishments, the organizers were humble. Sitting side by side at the table, they took turns making statements and answering questions. The klieg lights glimmered with feverish intensity, casting a harsh glare on their cold, pale faces. Cameras clicked and whirred; those of us with note pads scribbled furiously.

In a gravelly baritone, Birgil Kills Straight declared that the Lakota people had turned a new page in their history with the completion of the ride. "There's no message we're sending to the federal government by our actions," he cautioned. "What we did this week is part of an internal healing process."

He then went on to sketch the genesis of the ride. In the summer of 1985, a spiritual man named Curtis Kills Rees went on a vision quest, from which he returned with precise instructions for the Big Foot Ride. At about the same time, the organizers began to have their own dreams—dreams of horses and riders and hoops bedecked with eagle feathers, sacred dreams full of signs and portents. "We've been planning this ride for a long time," Birgil said. He then mentioned Black Elk's prediction that, in the aftermath of what had occurred at Wounded Knee, it would take seven generations to mend the sacred hoop of the Lakota Nation. That seventh generation, in the presence of youngsters such as little Josh, had now made its appearance.

Arvol Looking Horse spoke about the pipe. The pipe was given to the people way back in the misty dawn of time by White Buffalo Calf Woman. It provides the link between the temporal and the spiritual. It represents the means by which the people can come into contact with all that is *wakan* in the universe. It possesses consummate power and must be treated with respect. Periodically, when the people fail to behave according to the ideals embodied by the pipe, it is put away, out of sight. Such an event occurred in 1980, in the wake of the 1973 Wounded Knee uprising, when murder, arson, and violence rocked Pine Ridge and the other reservations. For seven years the pipe was kept from view. In a hesitant voice, not looking at the cameras but rather down at his splay-fingered hands floating out to either side of the microphone, Arvol added that by 1987 the climate on the reservations had sufficiently improved to warrant the pipe's unveiling.

Ron McNeill, looking nifty in a black kerchief and wide-brimmed black hat, offered reporters a quick history lesson. As a result of a series of fraudulent treaties in the 1880s, the great Sioux Nation had been carved up into nine separate reservations. The purpose of the breakup was to disrupt communication, destroy the people's cohesiveness, and dilute their power. "By our actions this week, we have taken a small but significant step toward bringing these different factions back together again."

Alex White Plume cited the positive changes that had taken place among the Lakota since the mid-1970s. More people were speaking the language. More ceremonies were being performed. Lakota history and culture were being emphasized in the schools. People were taking pride in being Indian. "One of the lessons we can all learn from the ride is how to be humble, how to be a follower, how to be a common person, how to make ourselves worthy of the spirit of the sacred pipe."

Alex explained how each day of the ride had been dedicated to a different aspect of Lakota society: first day, orphans; second day, the elderly; third day, the sick and infirm; fourth day, prisoners; fifth day, women. Special prayers and tributes were directed to each subject during that day.

"We acknowledge the superiority of women in our culture," Alex said. "Our greatest artifact, the pipe, was brought to us by White Buffalo Calf Woman. White Buffalo Calf Woman also taught us how to perform our other ceremonies, including the Wiping of the Tears, which we will observe tomorrow morning at the grave site."

Jim Garrett, a trained ecologist, a man with a solid scientific background, spoke in traditional Lakota fashion, almost exclusively in descriptive images. "Just as a cloud between a husband and wife can cast a shadow upon their marriage, so does the pollution we generate as human beings cast a shadow between the marriage of the sun and earth. We are all in relationship with every living thing. How can we offer our best when the bad things get in the way and obstruct our willingness to let the best shine forth?"

Cameras rolled; shutters snapped; high-tech recorders captured the subtlest voiceprints. Those of us with pencils dutifully copied down memorable turns of phrase. Afterward, in Bob's car, plowing through the pitch-black night back to Kyle and the Little Wound School, we mulled over the meaning of it all. "It's impossible to distill the significance of the week's activities in a few pithy phrases," Bob said. The glow of the dashboard lights reflected off his bearded cheeks. "The experience can't be categorized. I can see why the organizers had a tough time deciding whether to include the media in the final ride. You hate to see the experience oversimplified, at the same time you want to get the word out. You want people to know about the story, even if you know they can't understand it all."

The headlights cut a puny swath through the spooky darkness. So black was the night that nothing—not a fence, not the round form of a hill—could be seen outside the beam the lights projected. Bo had been silent since we left Manderson. Suddenly he spoke up. "We don't have any business here." His voice was clipped. The faint Dutch accent was detectable under the strain of speaking in a foreign tongue. "None of us. We're curious, we're sincere, we want to help, but we don't belong. We don't have a clue. We don't know how these people feel, and when we try and explain their feelings to a non-Indian audience, we get it wrong. We do them a disservice. Only they know how they feel, and if they choose not to say anything, it's their business. The age of the anthropologist is over."

"You just talked yourself out of a job," Bob said gently, "and me, and him." He jerked his thumb at the back seat where I sat, still feeling the cold, staring out the window.

"I know," Bo whispered. He rolled a cigarette in the dim glow of the dashboard lights. He put the cigarette between his lips and left it there, unlit.

We reached the grave site the following morning around nine. Despite the dangerous cold, a crowd had already assembled. The cold was like the edge of a sheet of razor-sharp metal. I thought I had experienced the ultimate in freezing weather yesterday, but the cold this final morning, December 29, was more extreme than anything I had encountered all week. It was impossible to remain outdoors for more than a few minutes. Fortunately, the basement of the Sacred Heart Catholic Church, located behind the grave site, was open, and when standing outside became intolerable, we could dive down the steps and join the throng in the basement drinking hot coffee and eating donuts. Someone said that, with the wind chill, the temperature was eighty below. The number seemed meaningless. The cold was blinding. It was paralyzing. It was vicious enough to kill. Surfacing from the basement warmth to the front steps of the church (early morning mass had been completed, but few of the parishioners bothered to stir from their comfortable pews), the cold struck like a vacuum, sucking the air from the lungs, making it difficult to breathe. Standing outdoors was like being immured in a solid wall of ice. As we waited for the riders to appear, we jumped up and down and flapped our arms. Though the cold kept away a lot of older people, by 10:30 the yard between the church and graveyard was packed with onlookers.

Standing in the yard, with the wind snarling and slicing, we could do little more than stamp our feet and swing our arms. By 10:45 a few trailers pulled up to the foot of the knoll, at approximately the same place where, a hundred years earlier, the Seventh Cavalry had established their bivouac. Draped with blankets, padded with quilts, the horses emerged reluctantly into the wind, looking withered, compressed to puny figures by the awful weight of the cold. As the riders saddled up, a distinguished elder named Bill Horn Cloud gave an invocation in Lakota over a bullhorn. The old man's voice hung in the air like a length of frozen clothesline, breaking off into brittle pieces as he completed the prayer.

An unmarked car brought South Dakota governor George Mickelson from the Pine Ridge airport, and after sitting incognito off to one side for a while, he decided to pay his respects at the grave site before the riders came up the hill and the ceremonies began. He levered himself out of the snug comfort of the idling car and ambled stiffly up the path. He was a tall man, wearing a handsome overcoat and a Russian-style hat with ear flaps. People in that portion of the yard milled about, watching. I was standing on the church steps with Dana and missed what happened next. (Bob Keyes gave me the details.) A contingent of AIM members, with Russell Means prominent in the foreground, stood at the hinged gate that offered passage through a flimsy wire fence into the grave site. When Mickelson tried to advance, Russell drew himself up and blocked the way. Though bundled in a hat and scarf, his face was lit with a ferocious scowl. Flanking Russell were several tough-looking lieutenants. Bob didn't catch the exact exchange of dialogue. Words were bandied back and forth. When it was over, Mickelson's shoulders under his expensive coat sagged a notch or two; he turned and walked back to the car. To Bob Keyes, leaning through the open window a few moments later, he said, "Means physically restrained me from going into the graveyard. He's grandstanding, just like he always does. He said I wasn't welcome here. I asked him who he was."

Word of Means's rebuff quickly circulated through the crowd. Of all the incidents that ruffled the otherwise harmonious week, this was the most discordant. The reaction on the part of several Indians I spoke to was anger and frustration. "Means had no right to do that," a young man growled. "I really don't like the son of a bitch. This is supposed to be a healing ceremony for people of every color. That kind of rudeness is inexcusable."

At last the riders plodded up the hill, only a few score, considerably fewer than the number that rode into Wounded Knee yesterday afternoon. They circled the grave site in a clockwise motion and reined in their horses. The excruciating cold prompted the organizers to abbreviate the Wiping of the Tears Ceremony to a shorter observance known as the Feeding of the Spirits. The body of riders lined up parallel to the wire fence on the west side of the grave site blocked the view for those of us standing on the church steps. With a shove from several pairs of hands, I climbed onto the porch railing. A quartet of spiritual leaders stood in front of the monument inside the sturdy wire fence that wrapped around the grave site; one of the men clutched a pipe, and he was praying in a barely audible voice. The crowd lapsed into numbed silence. Horses snorted and stamped. The wind hissed and fumed. It was virtually impossible to look face-on into the full brunt of that scourging cold; exposed to the wind, those along the south arc of the circle, facing in the same direction as the spiritual leaders, sat immobile on their horses like stone statues, their heads bowed. The pain accompanying those gruesome blasts, for me at least, blocked out whatever reverential thoughts I needed to feel. When I looked up again, the ceremony was over. At a signal from the man with the pipe, the horses thunked to the left and down the hill. The crowd began to break up and head for their vehicles or back into the comfort of the church. A few minutes later, like a man whose joints have been soldered together out of rusty steel, I walked alone through the hinged gate and along a wire fence skirting the grave-site's south perimeter. The base of the monument inscribed with the names of the Miniconjou victims was covered with offerings: bananas, oranges, *wasna*, tobacco, apples, fry bread. Tobacco ties and clusters of directional flags fluttered along the wire fence. An old man, hatless, white haired, bearing the unmistakable face of a full blood, scattered a coffee can full of ashes against the monument's foundation. The wind skirled the ashes in a tight circle, then skirled them around again, this time in a looser circle, a foot or two higher in the air. Then, aloft in a trailing line, the ashes, still circling, thinning to a tail of microscopic specks, disappeared into the bitter air.

It was time to think about my car. I had left it at Dooch Clifford's house on the outskirts of Manderson. Most likely the engine had frozen solid, though Dooch had promised to drive it now and then. Dooch's house was located at the foot of an outcropping of prominent bluffs. Dooch's wife, Pinky Plume, owned a store in Manderson. Pinky's store was a gathering place, a clearing house, a nerve center for the latest reservation information. A tall, attractive, full-figured woman, Pinky was always helping to organize an activity to benefit the people of her district; her generosity extended to the menagerie of animals she and Dooch sheltered on their property.

Dooch had driven the car a time or two, though after the weather we had experienced, I fully expected the car never to start again. A compact, broad-shouldered man, Dooch labored inside the open hood for half an hour, juicing the frozen battery with cables attached to his pickup, treading the accelerator with a delicate touch. Urrr, urrr, urrr, cough, sputter, wheeze, urrr, urrr, urrr—finally, miraculously, there was a rheumy hum as the engine turned over and grumbled into action. I skipped around the back bumper, flouncing my heels. A satisfied grin split Dooch's generous face. As if on cue, a flock of geese came waddling out of a ramshackle shed, quacking and fussing. Dooch paused to stroke their sleek heads; then, like an impresario at the close of a successful performance, he slowly lowered the hood.

With the car running and the heater at full blast, I drove into Manderson for a final stop at Pinky's store. The place was filled with people who had attended the grave-site ceremonies; I circulated, listening to stories. A number of people had boycotted the observance out of fear of the cold, the shenanigans of Russell Means, the likelihood of a media circus. Rippling like a troublesome leitmotif through the week's activities was the suspicion that the Big Foot Ride might somehow be subjected to the wrong kind of publicity. The suspicion was legitimate; many times the media had come to Pine Ridge saying they wanted to report the latest news, only to report the old news—poverty, alcoholism, poor housing—standard clichés which muddy the public perception of contemporary Indian reservation life and patently ignore the positive developments taking place there.

Pinky was in her glory behind the counter, kibitzing, making change, handing out candy from the glass jars she kept by the register. I talked to John Steele, a councilman from the Wounded Knee district, who the following year would be elected chairman of the tribal council; John's wife worked as a clerk in Pinky's store. With him was Ted Hamilton, librarian at Oglala Lakota College. Neither man had been on the ride, though they had followed the day by day progress with keen interest.

"This is a great day for the Lakota Nation," Steele declared. "If we could have this spirit every day on the reservation, we could solve all our problems."

"Which problems are worst?" I asked.

"Unemployment." He shook his head. "The population of Pine Ridge is about twenty-two thousand. Half that number is probably employable, though at its peak the job market has only about twenty-five hundred positions available. That makes it tough. Wintertime, like now, we suffer 85 to 90 percent unemployment." His intelligent face behind the dark frames of his glasses winced perceptibly. "People want to live here. They want to raise their children here. It's their land. It's where their ancestors are buried. Why can't we become more self-sufficient? We need to attract light industry. We need to establish our own credit houses. We need to encourage tourism."

He looked at Ted Hamilton, who was nodding vigorously.

"This is a great day. I tell you something. Things will never be the same after this ride. We're mending the broken hoop that Black Elk spoke about. The seventh generation has come full circle."

By seven o'clock that evening the gymnasium of the Little Wound School began to fill up. People streamed through the front doors and down the steps onto the polished hardwood floor. Entire families, young and old, carrying folding chairs, water bottles, sacks and coolers packed with food, bundled in winter clothes, their eyes glazed with the cold, shuffled on snow-booted feet, smelling like stale Popsicles forgotten at the back of a freezer. Bow-legged men in high-crowned Stetsons with silver belt buckles, wearing long johns and wool shirts buttoned at the throat, sauntered across the floor accompanied by diminutive women with wizened faces and sleek gray hair, clutching baggy purses and leaning on the supportive arms of sons and daughters. Cavorting with manic energy, pantomiming jump shots as they passed under the basketball nets, came dark-haired, black-eyed children. Into the portable bleachers, which on both sides of the cavernous interior had been extended to their full length, the families filed, there to lay out blankets and cushions, there to unfold their portable chairs, there to remove their cumbersome outer wraps. The noise inside the high-ceilinged room rose like a water level. It was *wacipi* time—time to powwow, time to celebrate the completion of a momentous week.

Dancers in feathered costumes glided across the floor, their bodies shimmering; tiny bells and turtle-shell clappers attached to their legs and arms alternately jingled and clacked. Some wore single feathers in their hair; others wore elaborate headdresses. The men were bare chested; their muscular torsos were splashed with ceremonial paint. The women were garbed in exquisite dresses with fringed sleeves, which flowed well past their knees; the hems were embroidered with multicolored beads. Soft moccasins covered their feet; breastplates latticed with creamy porcupine quills dangled from their necks. All the dancers carried themselves with special dignity and grace, including the children, dressed up in their own elaborate costumes.

Accompanying the dancers, togged out in matching sweatshirts and windbreakers bearing their own special logos, were teams of drummers from reservations all over South Dakota. The drums they toted were as big as tractor wheels. The men carried them flat, like huge platters, raised high over their heads. Settled in the corners of the gym, they pulled up chairs and sat down and began testing their leather-tipped sticks against the taut membranes. Like the dancers, the drummers wore their hair long, showering down to their shoulders or tied in pony tails. Mostly they were young guys in their teens and twenties, with a sprinkling of middle-aged uncles, fathers, and cousins.

At the west end of the gym, along the top of a platform, was a line of tables. At the center stood a dais equipped with a microphone. A fellow in a Levi jacket and cowboy hat barked numbers through the PA system, accompanied by a flurry of electronic bleeps. Out of this bedlam at some point during the evening a drum and dance contest would be staged, after which the Wiping of the Tears Ceremony would be performed in its entirety. The atmosphere inside the congested gym was charged and expectant. Bo, Sherry, Dana, and I sat high in the bleachers, looking down on the activity. Outside, it was forty below; inside, it was comfortable and warm.

Around 7:30, with a crash of drumbeats, the dancing began. Splendidly costumed men paraded to the center of the court where, in time to the staccato pulse, they commenced to shimmy with sinuous ease. The vigor they displayed was remarkable—forceful foot-stomping, bird-like bobbing, compact body whirls, rapid ducking and weaving—so different from the slow, gravid, downward shuffle of the Hopi dancers I had seen in Arizona. The Hopis clawed with their toes at the earth like badgers, as if trying to dig a hole, whereas the Lakota jerked and strutted and preened, exploding straight into the air with the agility of prairie chickens.

The women were fluid and composed, incarnations of the modesty and refinement that lie at the heart of Lakota femininity. Their loose dresses, flowing well past the knees, were marvels of decorative art. Fringed with buckskin, stitched with beads, bedizened with sequins, they flashed in the overhead lights with an iridescent luster. Fancy adornments of quill work graced their dresses, an art form, once though to be lost, that has made a comeback in recent times. The highlight of the female performers was a jingle dancer—a young woman, quite pretty, tall and rangy, with rippling arms and a shapely figure. Her dress was encrusted with scores of tiny bells arranged in concentric bands from her neck all the way down to the hem of her skirt. As she swayed and dipped through a series of complicated steps, the dress gave off a ringing tintinnabulation that could be heard over the steady throb of the drums.

Dancing and drumming lie at the heart of Lakota culture. The shape of the drum configures the shape of the earth; the pounding of the leather tympanum generates a beat that embodies the rhythmic pulse of the cosmos. Such a powerful spectacle was bound to attract the attention of federal authorities after the Indians were confined to the reservations; once the Ghost Dance furor died down, dancing on the reservations was either outlawed or restricted. In 1923, the Commissioner of Indian Affairs decreed that dancing could be held only during the summer months. In an effort to wean young people away from its pernicious influence, no one under the age of fifty was permitted to attend a powwow. Towns adjoining the reservations were cautioned not to encourage dancing, much to the disgruntlement of the local merchants who recognized its value as an entertainment draw. Missionaries and government employees were instructed to discourage the barbaric practice, in hopes of improving "the moral welfare of the Indian." In 1934, the Indian Reorganization Act officially rescinded this repressive policy, and since then the *wacipi* has bounded back to the crest of popularity it enjoys today.

Two nights ago, on this same floor, a group of elders had performed a round dance. The round dance is a simple step that seems to involve little more than joining hands and moving clockwise with a funny little kick-like motion. After the elders finished, and before we really knew what was happening, the emcee over the PA system announced that he wanted to see the white male representatives of the national and international media assemble in the center of the floor for a round dance. I got caught before I could make it to the men's lavatory to conceal myself; so did Bo and Bob Keyes and a bunch of photographers. Twelve of us formed a ragged circle at the tip-off line; to the steady beat of a drum, we gyrated to the left, trying to imitate the graceful movements of the elders. But a dozen white boys in winter pants and wool stockings simply couldn't cut the motion. As the drum boomed, we lurched and staggered, much to the amusement of the Indians in the audience (and the female members of the national and international media), who reared back in their bleacher seats and roared. Bewildered and embarrassed, the twelve of us lost all semblance of decorum and fell into spasmodic fits of shucking and jiving, as if we were listening to Chuck Berry at a sock hop back in the high-school auditoriums of our youth. The Indians were convulsed. They hooted and clapped their hands and wiped the tears that leaked from their eyes. Like windup toys gone berserk, the twelve of us continued to bang against one another until the drumming mercifully ceased and the emcee between choking fits of laughter begged us to stop.

The evening wound on. More people appeared. By nine o'clock, when the Wiping of the Tears Ceremony began, every row of the double set of portable bleachers was occupied. Down on the floor, dozens of elders had made themselves comfortable in folding chairs. Shortly after nine, a call went out for everyone who had participated in the Big Foot Ride to come down to the floor. All my buddies descended, but I hesitated. Yes, I had as much right as any other non-native to take part, but something in me elected to maintain my identity as a witness. I wanted to savor the spectacle from the perspective of an outsider looking in. Halfway down the bleacher steps, Dana looked back at me, but I shook my head. For the moment, I was where I needed to be.

The circle containing the participants that finally came together covered the entire perimeter of the basketball court. Wilmer Stampede with two assistants walked around the inside holding bags of tobacco. Other assistants followed, passing out *wasna*. With everyone in possession of a fingerful of *wasna* and a pinch of tobacco, Wilmer and his assistants made their way around again with a bucket of water and a dipper. There were at least two hundred people in the circle, and it took awhile to give them all the opportunity to drink from the dipper. Before conducting the ceremony, Wilmer prayed; an hour later, after the circuit had been completed, he prayed again. There was no pop of flashbulbs; all cameras mounted on tripods were capped and turned toward the floor. What we were observing was *wakan;* it was also deeply stirring to everyone who had participated in the events of the past week. At the press conference the evening before, Jim Garrett had said that the fact that the spirits of the Wounded Knee victims had never been put to rest had been a cause of chronic turmoil among the people. The purpose of the ceremony this evening was to administer that long overdue relief. The grave site this morning had been the appropriate place, but the cold had intervened, though that in its own way was fitting, as it was out of the North that the harsh, cleansing winds were thought to blow. The ceremony this evening in the high-school gymnasium was appropriately solemn. A child or two squalled, though for the most part the atmosphere was hushed. Those of us in the bleachers were on our feet, heads bowed. A tingling sensation teased the crown of my skull, all the way to the tips of my fingers.

And then the drums tucked away in the corners erupted again, a thunderous sound, and the circle transformed itself, folding into a double helix of revolving lines similar to the one that had formed that first night at the Takini School. The lines were contiguous at both ends, enabling people to reach out and shake hands as they passed. At the head of the line, prominent and dignified, accompanied by their wives and children, trailing behind the sacred hoop carried by Arvol Looking Horse, were the organizers. Behind them, cloaked in skins and quilted jackets, eagle feathers tied prominently to their hair, were the nineteen original riders. Behind them was a contingent of elders and full bloods, followed by Dennis Banks and Russell Means and the AIM delegation, followed by the Japanese and George White Thunder and the people I had come to know, followed by riders and walkers whose faces I recognized, followed by people whose faces I didn't. The drums throbbed and crashed. The singers wailed a melancholy plaint. The emotion that all evening had been gathering momentum inside my body reached a swelling crescendo.

With a stately motion, the two lines curled toward one another, touching lightly, sliding with snake-like ease in opposite directions, before curling back to make contact again. Though covering every square foot of the wide gymnasium floor, the pattern of the dancers from my perspective looked tight and interlocking. The tempo of the pounding drums increased. The singers cried with blood-curdling fervor. The sight was mesmeric. It seemed as if the entire Lakota Nation was weaving serpentinely in a slow, steady stutter-step across the floor. The fluidity of the lines was a marvel to behold, the inner face of one line sliding along the outer face of the other in a gentle, caressing motion. The two loops were like the complementary lobes of a single heart, pulsating and arterial, circulating energy, recharging it, thrusting it back into the air.

Derek Adams, back in the pack with the Japanese, bolted from the line and came skipping up the bleacher steps. "Come down here and join us!" he shouted to me. "You belong down here with us!"

I plunged down the steps and squeezed across the crowded floor and slipped between him and Dana Garber. Dana's blond face was flushed a lovely melon color. Her eyes glowed with pleasure. As we passed the head of the other line, I found myself shaking a succession of extended hands, looking into a succession of rapt, shining faces. I felt part of a living organism, absorbed in the currents of a mysterious emotion that was as powerful as anything I have ever experienced. The slug of drums rose off the hardwood floor, through my legs and stomach, striking with solid comfort against the muscle of my heart. Buoyed by the sound, transported by the high-pitched voices, the people in the two lines—myself happily among them—wove with elaborate courtesy in and out of one another's grasp, circling, circling. Circling.

Bibliography

Ambrose, Stephen E. *Crazy Horse and Custer: The Parallel Lives of Two American Warriors.* New York: New American Library, 1975.

Brown, Dee. *Bury My Heart at Wounded Knee.* New York: Holt, Rinehart & Winston, 1970.

Brown, Joseph Epes. *The Sacred Pipe: Black Elk's Account of the Seven Rites of the Oglala Sioux.* Norman: University of Oklahoma Press, 1953.

Byrd, Sidney H. "The Betrayal at Wounded Knee Creek." *Indian Country Today,* December 31, 1992.

Connell, Evan S. *Son of the Morning Star.* San Francisco: North Point Press, 1984.

Crow Dog, Mary. *Lakota Woman.* New York: Grove Weidenfeld, 1990.

Danker, Donald F. "The Wounded Knee Interviews of Eli S. Ricker." *Nebraska History* 62 (1981): 151–243.

DeMallie, Raymond J., and Douglas R. Parks, ed. *Sioux Indian Religion.* Norman: University of Oklahoma Press, 1987.

Dooling, D. M., ed. *The Sons of the Wind: The Sacred Stories of the Lakota.* New York: Parabola Books, 1984.

Eastman, Charles A. (Ohiyesa). *From the Deep Woods to Civilization.* Lincoln: University of Nebraska Press, 1977.

Eastman, Elaine Goodale. *Sister to the Sioux.* Lincoln: University of Nebraska Press, 1975.

Hall, Philip S. *To Have This Land: The Nature of Indian/White Relations in South Dakota, 1888–1891.* Vermillion: University of South Dakota Press, 1991.

Hassrick, Royal B. *The Sioux: Life and Customs of a Warrior Society.* Norman: University of Oklahoma Press, 1964.

Hyde, George E. *Red Cloud's Folk: A History of the Oglala Sioux Indians.* Norman: University of Oklahoma Press, 1937.

———. *A Sioux Chronicle.* Norman: University of Oklahoma Press, 1956.

———. *Spotted Tail's Folk: A History of the Brule Sioux.* Norman: University of Oklahoma Press, 1961.

Jackson, Donald. *Custer's Gold: The United States Cavalry Expedition of 1874.* Lincoln: University of Nebraska Press, 1972.

Jensen, Richard E., R. Eli Paul, and John E. Carter, ed. *Eyewitness at Wounded Knee.* Lincoln: University of Nebraska Press, 1991.

Josephy, Alvin M., Jr. *The Patriot Chiefs.* New York: The Viking Press, 1958.

————. *Now That the Buffalo's Gone: A Study of Today's American Indians.* New York: Alfred A. Knopf, 1982

Josephy, Alvin M., Jr., Trudy Thomas, and Jeanne Elder. *Wounded Knee: Lest We Forget.* Cody, Wyo.: Buffalo Bill Historical Center, 1990.

Kadlecek, Edward and Mabell. *To Kill an Eagle: Indian Views on the Last Days of Crazy Horse.* Boulder, Colo.: Johnson Books, 1981.

Kolbenschlag, George R. *A Whirlwind Passes: News Correspondents and the Sioux Indian Disturbances of 1890–91.* Vermillion: University of South Dakota Press, 1990.

Lazarus, Edward. *Black Hills/White Justice: The Sioux Nation versus the United States, 1775 to the Present.* New York: HarperCollins, 1991.

Lewis, Thomas H. *The Medicine Men: Oglala Sioux Ceremony and Healing.* Lincoln: University of Nebraska Press, 1982.

Mails, Thomas E. *Fools Crow.* New York: Avon Books, 1980.

————. *Fools Crow: Wisdom and Power.* Tulsa, Okla.: Council Oak Books, 1991.

Matthiessen, Peter. *In the Spirit of Crazy Horse.* New York: The Viking Press, 1983.

McFeely, William S. *Grant: A Biography.* New York: W. W. Norton, 1981.

McGillycuddy, Julia B. *Blood on the Moon: Valentine McGillycuddy and the Sioux.* Lincoln: University of Nebraska Press, 1990.

McGregor, James H. *The Wounded Knee Massacre: From the Viewpoint of the Sioux.* Rapid City, S. Dak.: Fenske Printing Co., 1940.

Miles, Gen. Nelson A. *Serving the Republic.* New York: Harper & Brothers, 1911.

Miller, David Humphreys. *Ghost Dance.* New York: Duel Sloan and Pearce. 1959.

Mooney, James. *The Ghost Dance Religion and the Sioux Outbreak of 1890.* Lincoln: University of Nebraska Press. 1991.

Neihardt, John G. *Black Elk Speaks.* Lincoln: University of Nebraska Press, 1961.

Nelson, Bruce. *Land of the Dacotahs.* Minneapolis: University of Minnesota Press, 1946.

Olson, James C. *Red Cloud and the Sioux Problem.* Lincoln: University of Nebraska Press, 1965.

Powers, William K. *Oglala Religion: Tradition and Innovation.* Lincoln: University of Nebraska Press, 1975.

————. *Yuwipi: Vision and Experience in Oglala Ritual.* Lincoln: University of Nebraska Press, 1982.

Rosa, Joseph G., and Robin May. *Buffalo Bill and His Wild West: A Pictorial Biography.* Lawrence: University Press of Kansas, 1989.

Ross, Dr. A. C. *Mitakuye Oyasin.* Fort Yates, N. Dak.: Bear Publishers, 1989.

Sandoz, Mari. *Crazy Horse.* Lincoln: University of Nebraska Press, 1942.

————. *Love Song to the Plains.* Lincoln: University of Nebraska Press, 1961.

————. *These Were the Sioux.* New York: Hastings House, 1961.

Smith, Rex Alan. *Moon of Popping Trees.* Lincoln: University of Nebraska Press, 1975.

Steltenkamp, Michael F. *Black Elk: Holy Man of the Oglalas.* Norman: University of Oklahoma Press. 1993.

Symthe, Donald. *Guerrilla Warrior: The Early Life of John J. Pershing.* New York: Charles Scribner's Sons, 1973.

Utley, Robert M. *The Last Days of the Sioux Nation.* New Haven, Conn.: Yale University Press, 1963.

————. *Frontiersmen in Blue: The United States Army and the Indian, 1848–1865.* New York: Macmillan, 1967.

————. *Frontier Regulars: The United States Army and the Indian, 1866–1891.* New York: Macmillian, 1973.

————. *The Lance and the Shield: The Life and Times of Sitting Bull.* New York: Ballantine, 1994.

Utter, Jack, ed. *Wounded Knee and the Ghost Dance Tragedy.* Lake Ann, Mich.: National Woodlands Publishing Co., 1991.

Vestal, Stanley. *Sitting Bull: Champion of the Sioux.* Norman: University of Oklahoma Press, 1957.

Walker, James R. *Lakota Myth.* Lincoln: University of Nebraska Press, 1983.

————. *Lakota Society.* Lincoln: University of Nebraska Press, 1992.

Welch, James. *Killing Custer: The Battle of the Little Big Horn and the Fate of the Plains Indians.* New York: W. W. Norton, 1994.